Vikram Seth's
The Golden Gate

Vikram Seth's
The Golden Gate

Edited by

S. Ramaswamy

Prestige Books International
New Delhi

Published by
Prestige Books International
New Delhi 110060
prestigebooks@gmail.com

Associate Office
60/29-45 Parramatta Road,
Concord, NSW 2137
Australia

ISBN: 978-93-82186-12-0

Printed in India

Contents

Acknowledgements

My first debt of gratitude is to Dr. R.K. Dhawan who asked me to prepare this book. Since my retirement fifteen years ago I had not been in touch with my erstwhile colleagues and old students. I welcomed this golden opportunity to re-open the gate of my friendship through requesting them to write articles on *The Golden Gate* and they were ever so kind and gracious to oblige me. My affectionate and sincere gratitude to all of them: Professor L.V. Shanthakumari, Retired Professor of English, for Chapterwise Critical Analysis of *The Golden Gate*; Professor S. Krishna Sarma. Retired Professor of English, Nagarjuna University, Guntur, for "The Theme of 'Loneliness' in Vikram Seth's *The Golden Gate*"; Dr. Sahana Das, Professor of Communicative English, Mount Carmel College, Bangalore, for "The Narrative Technique in *The Golden Gate*"; Dr. M.A. Yadugiri, Retired Professor of English (Linguistics and Stylistics) Bangalore University and Dr. Geetha Bhasker, Reader in English (Language Studies), for "*The Golden Gate* discussed Stylistically while Vikram Seth Writes More Novels"; Dr. Saumitra Chakravarty, Professor of English and Principal, V.V.S. College, Bangalore, for "Alienation and Homecoming: A Comparative Study of *The Golden Gate* and *An Equal Music*"; Dr. Cherian Alexander, Professor and head, Department of English, St. Joseph's college, Bangalore, for "A Mozartian Debut: A Note on Music in Vikram Seth's *The Golden Gate*"; Ms. Rita Joshi, L.S.R. College, University of Delhi, for "Intertextuality in *The Golden Gate*"; Ms. Swati Priya, Res. Scholar at P.G Department of English, Tilka Manjhi Bhagalpur University, for "Crisis of Identity, Alienation, Aloofness, Loneliness and Death in *The Golden Gate*"; Sandhya Rao Mehta, Sultan Qaboos University, for *The Golden Gate* and *A Suitable Boy* as Expatriate Novels; Dr. Goparanjan Misra, S.B.R. Govt. Women's College, Berhampur, for "The Horizon of Vikram Seth's Fiction."

Finally, I am grateful to Dr. Suman Bala, University of Delhi, for her meticulous editing of the volume and overseeing the text. Also, I express my gratitude to Prestige Books International for bringing out the book so elegantly and expeditiously. I believe it is more than a publishing house; it is an institution.

Introduction: Vikram Seth's *The Golden Gate*: A Unique Novel

S. RAMASWAMY

The Golden Gate is a unique novel. Vikram Seth himself is a unique novelist among Indian writers in English. It is good to see how he is unique as an Indian novelist in English before *The Golden Gate* is analysed in detail. The best introduction to Seth is provided by himself in one of his sonnets in *The Golden Gate* because the whole of this novel, including the contents and the Dedication is in the form of sonnet. *The Golden Gate* is not only a novel in verse but it is only in sonnets—591 of them! plus three—the Dedication and Acknowledgements and Contents:

> The author, Vikram Seth, directed
> By Anne Freegood, his editor,
> To draft to vita, has selected
> The following salient facts for her:
> In '52, born in Calcutta.
> 8 lb. 1 oz. Was heard to utter
> First rhymes ('cat,' 'mat') at age of three.
> A student of demography
> And economics, he has written
> *From Heaven's Lake*, a travel book
> Based on a journey he took
> Through Sinkiang and Tibet. Unbitten
> At last by wanderlust and rhyme
> He keeps Pacific Standard Time

This is the first unique thing about Seth. I don't know any Indian writer in English who has written a whole novel in sonnets, that too, rejecting the 'tyrannical' pentameter and taking to tetrameter. Apart from anything else just for his contribution of the sonnet in English, he should justly be considered unique. Neither Sri Aurobindo, nor Vikram Seth have "scorned the sonnet" of Petrarch, Shakespeare, Milton and Wordsworth, but while in the hands of Sri Aurobindo the sonnet reached the Himalayan heights attaining the mystical sublimity of Gowri Shankara, in Vikram Seth it not only comes down to the Californian silicon valley but adopts the everyday language of the American lingo. The author of *The Suitable Boy,* who has still remained a suitable boy, has achieved a technical "tour de force,' what with his ease with diction, impeccable wit, effortless fluency, sharp tongue and an unimpeachable mastery over the sonnet morphology. The unique liberty he has taken with the sonnet is of a very different nature from that of Gerald Manley Hopkins in his 'curtal' sonnet and his 'Terrible Sonnets' with their codas. This is seen in a typical sonnet in *The Golden Gate*:

> A week ago, when I had finished
> Writing the chapter you've just read
> And with avidity undiminished
> Was charting out the course ahead,
> An editor—at a plush party
> (Well-wined,—provisio speechy, hearty)
> Hosted by (long-live!) Thomas Cook
> Where my Tibetan travel book
> Was honoured—seized my arm: 'Dear fellow,
> What's your next work?' 'A novel . . .' 'Great!'
> We hope that you, dear Mr. Seth—
> 'In verse,' I added. He turned yellow.
> 'How marvellously quaint,' he said
> And subsequently cut me dead. (100)

'Seth' rhyming himself with 'great' is coincidental and convenient for rhyme and not in the least immodest! It is for critics to make this pronouncement—especially now, after his achievement subsequent to his writing *The Golden Gate*. He says that his first rhymes were formed at the age of three. Like Alexander Pope, he 'lisped in numbers for the numbers came'! About the choice of the form of *The Golden Gate*, Seth himself says:

How do I justify this stanza?
These feminine rhymes? My wrinkled muse?
This whole passé extravaganza?
How can I (careless of time) use
The dusty bread molds of Onegin
In the brave bakery of Regan?
The loves will surely fail to rise
Or else go stale before my eyes. (101)
Why, asks a friend, attempt tetrameter?
Because it once was noble, yet
Capers before the proud pentameter,
Tyrant of English. . . . 5-4 (102)

To return to the theme of uniqueness of Seth among Indian writers in English, it may be remembered that the novel in verse, though the immediate inspiration of Seth is the Russian writer Pushkin and the novel is *Eugene Onegin* as acknowledged by Seth in the above lines, the form 'Novel in Verse' itself has a history.

As early as the eleventh century, Kshemendra of Kashmir wrote two novels in Sanskrit, *Padyakadambari* and *Lavanyavdti*, Kshemendra was a well-known figure in the literary circles of his time. He was the Guru of princes and kings. Beginning with Jalhana (13th century) down to the present day he has been popular with Sanskrit anthologists. He was scholar, literary critic, humorist, wit and satirist. He was the one who gave the concept of 'Auchitya' which means appropriateness in literary composition—one of the basic ideas in Indian 'Theory.' Incidentally the word 'Kadambari' itself means a 'Novel' in Sanskrit. It happens to be the title of Bana's novel also. Kshemendra's *Lavanyavati* depicts the story of a courtesan Vasantika trying to seduce a Vedic scholar by name Atrivasu. Here is an erotic verse from it:

Stanau stabdhau tikshnam nayanayugalam nimnamudaram
Brhvorvakra vrittirvihitamunimarodharamanih |
Tathasanne daivadiyati vishame durjanagane
Guni madhye haarah sprishati tava dolatalatam ||

This is a description of the 'lavanya' or the graceful beauty of the heroine of the novel. If *Lavanyavati* is his own original work, Kshemendra's *Padya Kadambari* is a poetic transcreation of Bana's famous novel, *Kadambari*. Bana, the well-known author of *Harshacharita*, has also written the novel *Kadambari* which is one of the jewels of Sanskrit literature. Bana seems to have composed *Kadambari* in verse as well, which might have been lost even by the time of Kshemendra. However, it is Kshemendra's versification of Bana's classic novel in prose that we are concerned with here. Kshemendra himself seems to have had a good opinion of it to such an extent that he quotes from it to illustrate a point in literary criticism in his own work Kavikanthabharana. Here is a stanza just for the sake of illustration:

> Kinchitkunchitakamakarmukalatamaitri vichitra brhivo
> Narmoktissmithakantibhih kusumita pragalbhyagarbha girah |
> Ragotsanganishangibhi sarasatasamvadibhirvibhramai
> Rayushyam paramam taya ratipateh praptam mrigakshya vayah||

This rendering into verse the novel of Bana (606-646 A.D) has been referred to here, only in passing, to record that the form of a novel in verse did exist as a distinct genre in Sanskrit literature as early as the eleventh century, if not earlier.

I believe there is a novel in verse in Tamil entitled *Aathiyur Avathani* written by one Seshaiengar, published in Madras in 1875, the only copy of which is said to be in the British Museum, London! The inspiration for that novel is in the oral tradition and folk songs. I am given to understand that it is a social document and the locale is Aathiyur near Pondicherry and the immediate model for the novel was 'Desigu Rajan Kathai.' The characters are Vinayalan, with the title 'Avathani' who is the hero, Gandhari, Dronar, Devadatta, Kumudini, Azhikandan, Aahavazhi. This is being mentioned only as a curiosity item to remind that *The Golden Gate* is the only one of its kind in English. As I could not locate the Tamil text in the British Museum at London when I was there in 1983, I must confess that my information cannot be documented.

The uniqueness of Vikram Seth as an Indian writer in English can be established through Secondary Sources as well as his Interviews. The main thrust of my argument is that no other Indian writer in English has the range, width of experience, cosmopolitanism, eclecticism and an integrated view of the East and the West that he has. Let me illustrate. In addition to the Vita supplied by him, quoted above, at the beginning, a few more biographical details are necessary to follow the Tainian method of the Man, the Milieu and the Moment. His mother was India's first female Chief Justice. His background, academic as well as non-academic, is unique. He lived in London and went to school at Tonbridge aged 17, and was greatly interested in his origins. 'My family has been the biggest thing in my life,' he says in an Interview published in the *Guardian* in 2005 and re-published. Seth's aunt was a German Jew. About his *Two Lives* (Little, Brown) he says that it is "the first very personal, non-fictional thing I have written.' Seth's cosmopolitanism can be seen in the fact that he studied classical Chinese, learnt Mandarin, travelled in Sinkiang and Tibet and he even wrote a travelogue entitled *From Heaven's Lake*. Born in Calcutta,—he calls his mother 'an honorary Bengali'—he lives in Delhi. After studying in England and then for ten years in his twenties at Stanford in California, where he wrote his Pushkin-inspired poetic homage to San Francisco entitled *The Golden Gate*. The mathematical precision with which he has arranged the sonnets, suitably numbered to indicate the progress of the plot, such as it is, takes us to his interest in Mathematics. As he has said in an Interview: 'I love speculating about solutions to problems in mathematics. . . . I do look at chess and bridge problems in newspapers. I find that relaxing.' Considering the sheer volume of his output in addition to its incredible variety—his *A Suitable Boy* being the longest single-volume novel in Indian Writing in English is a record—he refers to himself as 'crippled by procrastination': 'I need my natural laziness to be counteracted by obsession in order to do anything. I became obsessive about calligraphy, for example and learned Mandarin.' Does he regret not finishing his Ph.D? 'Yes, I do.

But on the other hand, that particular year could not have been filled with *The Golden Gate* and my dissertation.' About his *Two Lives* Vikram Seth says: 'Most biographies are either about famous people—generals, politicians and so on—or they are memoirs.' *Two Lives* and *A Suitable Boy* before it reflects a personal story-telling philosophy that he actually sets down towards the end of the book: 'Behind every door, on every ordinary street, in every hut in every ordinary village on this middling planet of a trivial star, such riches are to be found. And I don't think that is being falsely democratic. There are interesting stories in everybody's lives. How well they are told, and whether they reflect their eras as truly as Shanti's or Henry's may vary. But they are there. We just have to look for them.'

In this introductory statement, Seth's views have been quoted from his 'interviews' as these provide an insight into his insights. He has said 'I get impatient with research, but it is important.' Yes indeed, research is important not only for a critic but for a creative writer too—certainly for a modern writer like Vikram Seth who has written a travelogue, a biography, conventional novels as well as a 'Novel in Verse' which is unique.

Works Cited

Vikram Seth. *The Golden Gate*. Oxford University Press. Delhi, Bombay, Calcutta, Madras. 1986.

Minor Works of Kshemendra, ed. Vidyaratna E.V.V. Raghavacharya and D.G. Padhye (The Sanskrit Academy, Osmania University, Hyderabad, 1961), p. 73, two stanzas quoted are transliterated into English, just to give a feel of the original Sanskrit.

Refer to verses quoted in the edition of Motilal Banarasidas, Varanasi, ed. Vaman Kesar Lele (1967). My transliteration.

The Hindu, Sunday, February 1, 1998, p. xv.

The Hindustan Times, Sunday May 2, 1999, p. 5.

The New Indian Express, Monday, July 28, 2003.

The Hindu, Sunday, September 25, 2005, Magazine, p. 5.

Sunday Herald, October 23, 2005, p. 7.

The New Sunday Express (*Views and Reviews*), October 23, 2005, p. 2.

The Golden Gate
Chapterwise Critical Analysis

SHANTHA KUMARI

The Golden Gate, by Vikram Seth is a unique achievement in the history of novel, as it is completely (wholly) composed only in sonnets. Even the acknowledgements and dedication are in sonnets. To match this effort of the author Penguin Books also has honoured this effort with a sonnet. 585 sonnets distributed unevenly in thirteen chapters, unfold the motif, plot and the character of the novel. [The number of the sonnets from the first chapter to the last contain 41, 57, 37, 53, 44, 45, 48, 37, 40, 40, 55, 36 and 52 respectively].

There are only six main characters, John, Janet, Phil, Liz, Sue, Ed; Paul (the kid), Liz's parents, Matt and Joan, Rowena, Chuck are minor characters. Claire, though the agent of Phil and Paul's loneliness does not appear in the novel. Charlemagne, Liz's cat, plays an important role, being a catalytic agent in bringing estrangement between John and Liz. All these form the warp and woof in the fabric of the story. While San Francisco and California provide an urban, sophisticated, neo-modern backdrop to the action of the novel, the farmhouses of Mr. Dorati, Matt and Joan's garden, offer a pastoral loveliness and naturalness, and thus provide a fine contrast. The time and locale of the story is the twentieth century America and the action of the story takes place in restaurants, apartments, farmhouses, the Golden Gate Park and in some other places. Vikram Seth familiarizes the reader with some ceremonies like olive picking, housewarming, thanksgiving also. Along with these, the story presents the peace march and the demonstration against nukes by the American citizens. Through the characters of Janet and Sue, music and sculpture are introduced. The main theme of the novel is, man-woman relationship; it also deals with dreams and disillusionments in these relationships. More than all these, the evocation of the essential loneliness of modern man, his inability to cope with that loneliness, stressful, mediocre, superficial mechanical, low key life style, seems to be the main preoccupation of the author. Men like John fail to confront their own inner self, they cannot come to terms with their inner void. Their struggle is to escape their own inner self, their own gaping inner emptiness [as the great philosopher J. Krishnamurthy has pointed out]. John, Jane, and Ed represent such lonely persons. They live comfortably, earn money more than needed, but are not happy, and thus they represent the modern malaise, which is a global phenomenon of the present day.

Though the novel is composed in sonnets, the language is racy, sometimes dialogues too. The story unfolds chronologically, through direct narration and in flashbacks here and there. Sometimes the author himself interferes as a single chorus. Starting from the depiction of John's loneliness, the story narrates his affair with Liz, the separation, Phil's broken marriage with Claire, Phil and Ed's homosexual affair and their separation and Phil and Liz's marriage. The death of Jane is an accident; John, who had found happiness in Jane, again becomes lonely, but is consoled by the words of Janet's spirit. Begun with the loneliness and melancholic thoughts of the protagonist John in the first sonnet, the novel ends with John's melancholic thoughts. The difference is that Janet is dead but John feels the presence of her spirit. He imagines he hears her voice:

I am with you John, you're not alone
Trust me, my friend there is the phone
It isn't me you are obeying
Pay what are your own heart's arrears
Now, clear your throat, and dry the tears.

With these lines the novel ends, perhaps what knowledge had eluded John, when Jane was living, might have dawned now after her death. He has to learn to "pay his own heart's arrears."

Chapter I

The author begins the novel in the epic manner, by invoking the Muse "To make start more swift than weighty," addresses the reader and commences, "Once upon a time, say circa 1980, there lived a man. His name was John" like a traditional story teller, though he is narrating the story of a contemporary man. The first chapter consisting forty one sonnets introduces John, aged twenty-six, respected, lonely, and walking across the Golden Gate Park. The title of the novel too is introduced in the first sonnet itself. This protagonist of the novel is sad and encircled by loneliness, melancholy and death. This young man of twenty-six leading a very comfortable life, earning well, considered a successful man thinks: "If I died who would be sad? Who'd weep? Who'd gloat? Who would be glad?" Through these thoughts the author in the very beginning of the novel introduces the main theme of the novel, loneliness and the melancholy that is caused by loneliness even at such a young and enthusiastic age. Moreover, everyone needs some love and care, without which one feels lost. John at present is deprived of these. He tries to divert his thoughts from this "dispiriting theme" to some worldly thoughts like "electronic circuiting," "orgates and andgates," "nanoseconds, "megabites" etc. yet "caught in the kelp of loneliness cries for help." As an American average man of the twentieth century, John does not lack any modern amenities. He is a civilized person with good taste, handsome with graceful manners, his appetite for work is abnormal, works in an established firm, a plastic name-tag hangs around his neck. He is not reckless with money, he jogs regularly, does not smoke, avoids heavy drinking and churchgoing. He reads so much that some of his friends say he is a "surrogate for thinking." Grey-eyed, blond-haired, aristocratic in height, his corporate stock is booming. This is the profile of John given by the author. What else needs to be jolly and contented? But John is not happy. "For all his Mahair, serge and tweed" he "senses his life has run to seed," he becomes more and more rich, and more and more sad.

Sitting in the Park John observes that the September showers have painted the hills with a new green. He looks at flowers and remembers his childhood at San Francisco. Friday night, perhaps the thought that Saturday and Sunday—being holidays—aggravate in him the sense of biting loneliness of the present, his sad mood brings the nostalgic memories of his childhood. His mother is dead, his English father, who retired in Kent, rarely answers the letter of his son. And "John feels a cold cost of self-pity" envelop him. To overcome this sense of loneliness and self-pity John wanders into an ice cream parlour, looks at the pair of high school lovers nibbling sugar cones by turns. John too decides to buy a double scoop. Wherever his eye falls, he sees people in twos and threes, he is the only one who is alone. So he comes home to be comforted by old "Beatles and pink floyed," "Girl and money." They bring him only frustration and annoyance. Bitten by loneliness he drinks beer, he feels what he needs is "A one way ticket to Ride—and soon. Across the side of the Moon." Thus John's frustration and pessimistic mood is revealed. He remembers now his college days, his friend Phil, Berkeley friends, the jokes they enjoyed, their fights and their double-datings. They had burnt their candles at both ends. After college days John began worshipping Mammon by concentrating on earning more and more money. Phil, John's intimate friend, who was also like this till now, recently has developed a new zest for peace marches, protestations against production of Nukes. John now is almost scared to call Phil, for political debate may colour their friendship. John remembers their "light comraderie, dark beer, double-dating" which have now vanished. Perhaps to revive these memories of the "Golden Bear," John phones Phil but gets no response. Then he remembers Janet Hayakawa, his former friend. John and Janet had parted on good terms to lead their own individual lives. Janet was a sculptor and a drummer in the band of liquid sheep. The sounds produced by this band is compared to a throttled yelp, Morse crossed with a pig's squeal for help. Janet's medium for sculpturing is bronze and iron. 'Three eggs,' 'An Adolescent Lion,' 'Clothed Nude' are some of her sculptures, but she has not yet got the attention or acclaim of critics. Vikram Seth's comments upon the attitude of the critics are worth pondering, with its half-seriousness and half-funny attitude. He writes about the critics "with smooth and blinkered savagery/ servile and suave, obsessed by fashion/ these chicken-hearted chicken shits/ jerk off their weak and venomous wits."

The theme of loneliness finds expression, and is explored in the delineation of Jane's character also. She tries not to be disheartened by adverse criticism of her art and involves more and more in her art. Living alone in her flat she finds companionship in her cats Cuff and Link. She too ruminates about the past. John had phoned Jane, but could only listen to the recorded message of the answering machine. So he tries to immerse himself in Hardy, Donne, and some other authors. However, when he listens to Jane's voice on the phone, his melancholy is lifted, they fix a lunch at 16th street, 'The Shee Ching' where the food is good. Monotony and loneliness are broken by this. This proves nothing can be a substitute for human friendship and companionship. The next day John waits for Jane but she is late, for she was doing a torso. Seth describes food and drinks elaborately. John and Jane exchange their thoughts while eating. John conveys his sadness, his loneliness to Jane as if they are his maladies, and asks her suggestion to ward these off: "What is the root of my neurosis? I die/ I faint, I sink." This is the climax of his neurosis. This is not only the problem of John, but of every modern man, bereft of the support of a strong base to feel firm and secure. Jane's solution to this is John should get a lover. Jane's manner of talking irritates John. Yet she succeeds in making him think in the right way. She asks him about the girls in his office. When she drinks she talks about the weirdest subjects like guys with guys, guys with animals (homosexual and other unnatural matings); finally she suggests advertising like "young handsome yuppie seeks" etc. She warns him, if he does not do this, he will be a lonely weeping man. (However this proves true at the end of the novel) These two go on talking endlessly, but when the waiter presents the bill they are compelled to leave the place. They take leave of each other.

Before starting the second chapter, it is good to take a look at the delineation of the characters like John, Jane, Ed, Liz and others. The depiction of these and some other characters of *The Golden Gate* need not be combined only to the American texture of life, calling it yuppie culture. The problem of rich people especially young, in the globalised context, the problem of the void and loneliness they feel inside and fail to confront and overcome, even amidst their external hyper activities, speedy boisterous life, parties, drinking bouts, entertainments is a universal one. Though they cope with external problems perfectly, they cannot face their inner self. To avoid this confrontation with the inner self, to face that inner emptiness, they indulge in all sorts of activities, yet fail to oust that inner void that haunts them like a dark devil. John, Jane, Ed are the male and female examples of those beings who feel essential loneliness and emptiness within, yet fail to ward it off. This aspect of the novel reminds one of the words of J. Krishnamurthy. He says a person to escape meeting his own self in a silent solitude, indulges in many external activities like smoking, reading, worshipping, watching films, meeting friends, except to be still and meet the still centre of his inner being.

The depiction of gay relationship between Phil and Ed is rather long and elaborate, yet, this is the depiction of a perennial pattern of companionship that has existed since the time of Plato. This straightforward delineation of man-man relationship, with the details of warm sentiments and emotions between the pair, throws light on the concepts of gay or lesbian marriages that are becoming popular at present. Phil is divorced, he is a father of six-year-old Paul. Yet he likes Ed and has sexual relation with him. Along with his gay relationship, Phil loves his child and participates in peace march. Further, he breaks off his relation with Ed and marries Liz, Ed's sister. Like John, Ed too feels loneliness. Added to that he is torn between his homosexual desire and sense of guilt and breach of religious code. On the contrary Phil not merely defends homosexuality but strongly justifies this relationship. To him, homosexual relation also is a form of love, a manner of expressing one's tender feelings towards a male companion. John, Jane, Ed remind one of Eliot's 'Hollowmen,' yet these are big achievers in the materialistic world.

Chapter II

The second chapter, consisting of 57 sonnets, narrates Janet's routine life, her writing ads for John, arrival of Billet dons, John's response, his meeting with three girls, including Liz, materialization of their love, etc.

Janet comes home after a strenuous drumming in the band. Her arm hurts, sleep eludes her, she gazes at the stars. Her cats are asleep. She feels lonely, decides to write some ads for John. It is already morning, but the ad-writing is not completed. The cats are already awake and are fed. Janet's composition of the ad, gives us an idea of the world of advertisement in the modern times, it takes us directly to the ads of matrimonial columns.

"Young handsome yuppie, 26,/ Straight forward, sociable but lonely/ Cannot believe that he's the only/ Well rounded and well meaning square/ Lusting for love, if you, out there/ Are friendly, female under 30/ Impulsive, fit and fun, let's Be rash—Box." By that time the cat puts its paw on the writing. Jane thinks, this print of paw will serve as a signature. However, the outcome of this ad is stupendous; there are 84 letters. Jane sends the letters to John. John feels furious and shouts on phone to Jane: "Your crazy ad was garbage in and garbage out." Infuriated with his talk with Jane concerning these letters he drives carelessly and speedily and gets a ticket by the traffic police. In the office John's boss has fired the services of an engineer, John's colleague. John's plea with the boss, to reinstate that engineer is refused. The author familiarizes the working system in the office and rush-hour traffic of megacities. "He drives back on Route 101/ Above the rush hour droves, commuting/ bumper to bumper horns are hooting/ anacondas of the road jungle glide in fast" when John looks back. While driving John looks at the display of various attractive ads like cigarette ad of shapely legs that make John start. He thinks about the danger of unmindful driving. "Beneath the slab John Brown is stowed/ He watched the ad not the road," this will be his epitaph if he is not careful. The two sonnets describing John's driving and the ads on the road unfold the modern world of ads, their sharp and brief language, tantalising pictures and pert comments, slogans, on current matters, e.g., "Hark for Jesus," "The President is a Lesbian spy," "Nuke the Nukes" etc.

The author questions: "Need John's life be so bug infested?" The bug that is infesting is loneliness, the mechanical and comfortable life, the stress and tensions of modern life. John is changed, what has brought this change, Seth writes: "Work and the syndrome of possessions/ Leave little time for life's digressions." Now he has no friends, "his politics have slowly and strongly rigidified." Being an emotional waif since a small boy, never getting his mother's love, John has clung to "Standards good or bad." Thinking upon his life, now, John does not see any harm in reading the letters. It offers a change also. Glancing through the letters while driving, John selects a quarter, which is "not too evidently pornographic." After coming home, he picks three from them and writes "three crisp and courtly notes" and waits. To all the other letters he sends a xeroxed copy of a sort of regret note informing that the writer of the letter—rather details—does not match with requirements. This process of ad, reply and response brings in a new element of change and expectations, anticipation and disappointments. Something happens to break the monotony. One girl accepts his invitation to visit the theatre, on Saturday. She is introduced as a "Wasp Blue Stocking." She comes with a shocking pink parasol. She bores John with her continuous talking on *Macbeth*. Throughout, she oozes jargons. John is so bored that he turns very pale, the lady says that John has turned "as white as the ghost of Banquo." And the first adventure ends without any profit. The letter of acceptance, with the photo of the writer Belinda Beale arrives on Saturday and John waits to take the girl to the theatre. The play to 'enjoy' is *Cat on a Hot Tin Roof.* The name of the play becomes symbolic here as in Tennessee Williams for John literally feels like a cat on the hot tin roof in the company of "amorous Belinda." The name Belinda reminds one of the coquetry of Belinda in Pope's mock heroic poem *The Rape of the Lock.* This Belinda's dexterous digits "engage in passionate Petri sage along John's thighs." Belinda's efforts to hook John then and there are described very frankly. John becomes so exasperated and embarrassed that he concocts a story of a wife waiting for him. Yet John has not lost his hope, he waits for the third adventure, but the third lady, Anne has to 'leave for San Francisco soon.' So that meeting does not materialize. John's comments on the first two girls are quite interesting, "Belinda would have combusted me to cinder/ And wasp stung me to learned death."

There remains the seventh letter, long, elaborate and self-explaining, that creates curiosity and interest in John. The writer is Elisabeth Dorati (Liz). Liz is a law graduate of Stanford Law School (last year's batch), she is much sought after a match by attorneys, she is friendly, well-rounded, good-looking. She visits her dad at weekends in his farm. Her dad Professor Dorati is a vineyard farmer, Liz's parents press her for marriage, but she prefers to live alone with her cat Charlemagne. She did have one or two affairs, but they were not serious and intimate enough to lead to marriage. Liz's parents and the farmhouse breathe a puff of fresh air into the urbanized monotonousness of the story. Liz's brother Ed, has not yet got a 'significant other.' Sue, Liz's sister, is also introduced, she is a cello player. The cat Charlemagne becomes a character in the novel, as he becomes the root cause of separation between John and Liz. Liz's extreme attachment to the cat causes unhappiness, intolerance, a sort of jealousy in John.

John prefers to meet Liz on Sunday during the morning. Their meeting, process of their intimacy, flourishing of their love is depicted dramatically, naturally and interestingly. John thinks that "She is lovely," Liz thinks, 'he is handsome.' Both of them talk together, say sorry together, feel a sort of confusion, and exchange their new-found feelings and emotions. When the duo is rapt in discussion, once Jane comes there, looking at their raptness, she quietly leaves unnoticed by them. Liz thinks of John as a charmer. When Liz mentions her cat John says it is "A wonderful cat." In this first stage of romance. Everything about the other partner seems to be wonderful and fascinating. They cannot believe that they have become so intimate. John's "tension admits a transient ease," by the soothing words of Liz and their physical union, in the flat of Liz. But the very next morning when John wakes up, he feels uncomfortable in that unfamiliar bed, and to aggravate this feeling, he spots Charlemagne on his feet. This increases his heartbeat. But their intimacy and love-making continue. The author says: "the loving pair has bit the apple of mortal knowledge" and they have begun to babble stupidly. He prefers to leave the lovers in their "Arcadia, Shangrila et al." In many instances Vikram Seth brings in literary allusions.

Chapter III

The third chapter begins with the author's intervention. By introducing Phil and Paul, the themes of parentage, rift in marriages, divorces are explored in this chapter. Paul is a boy of six years, his observation "Dad you're going bald" makes Phil brood upon his genes. Father and son enjoy the Californian beautiful, blue sky. Paul is mesmerized by a spider and wants to keep it as a pet. Slowly the story of Phil, Claire and Paul unfolds. After Claire left Phil has responsibility of Paul. Claire has not come to her child even on his birthday. Phil has left Datatronics and has not been yet placed anywhere. He is a loving father and consents to tell stories to Paul. "Chromiska's Glory," 'Three Apple Tarts' are narrated with many interventions by the child. But the child is bored. Phil ruminates about his love, marriage and separation with Claire. Now he realises a great truth: "Disfiguring is what dreams are made for/ A fool is bliss, what made me feel/ our rings were not soft gold but steel." Phil and Claire represent people who become disillusioned about each other after marriage, when the heat of passion, warmth of emotion are totally spent up and incompatibility springs up and the pair separate. But John and Liz separate even before the wedding is solemnized. Phil and Paul meet John and Liz in the concert, where Sue is a cello player. John does not like Schonberg though he enjoys Mozart, who is the "Prince of music makers." The author's love and preference for particular music finds expression here. He showers abundant praise on Mozart's music. According to John, Schonberg is an "ulcer generator," his music is "cerebral clatter," and that makes John writhe and intensely ill. In the interval John and Liz meet Phil and Paul. Liz invites Phil to House-warming on Friday night. Phil admires Liz, John is pleased.

Chapter IV

The fourth chapter describes the house warming of Liz, introduces Mrs. Dorati, Liz's mother, Professor Pratt and some other persons. While everything is going on smoothly, there is a rub. John's new suit is spoiled by the "squalid cat Charlemagne's piss." He begins to kick the table, Liz tries to console him, but John's pent up anger against the cat bursts out. He shouts: "That cat should be castrated." "The Liquid Sheep" begins its rant. Phil comes, but looking at Jane, he is upset, for Jane is Claire's friend. It is revealed that once Jane, Claire, John and Phil had double-dated. After Phil has divorced Claire, Jane does not like Phil. Ed is introduced to Phil, Sue also is there. Ed is always sad and melancholic and his sisters cannot fathom the reason for his sadness. When Ed is introduced to Phil, there is a sudden rise of emotion between the two, this ultimately ends in their sexual relationship.

The dialogue between John and Phil reveals that Phil the whizkid of computers, the author of the learned tract on guidance system, has blown up his career for dumb slogans. But to Phil they are not dumb slogans. He believes in picketing, peace marches and demonstrations against nukes. He feels that the world is out of joint (a reminder of *Hamlet*) and says that their actions give heart to the protesters. Phil picturizes the dangerous situation everyone on the world has to face today. He says: "Imagine that the first bombs found us/ Just as we are as here we stand, a glass of liquor in hand." Then everything ends. Even Van Gogh's sunflowers will be gone. The only thing that remains is the effect of radioactivity. Through the character of Phil and his discussions, Vikram Seth presents the themes of Nukes, effects of radiation, cold-wars, threat of destruction to the civilisation not only of America, but of the whole world, and the whole creation itself. Nothing, the trees, whales, birds, wolves can escape the effect of radiation. Phil compels John and all the people to "think, how the crown of earth's creation/ Will murder that which gave him birth/ ripping out the slow womb of earth." Phil thinks that this madness of atomic researches causing radiation must be stopped. Phil's passion and enthusiasm attracts Ed and he is introduced to Phil. Ed, who never feels "short of words" feels numb before Phil. According to Ed, there are two passwords, one is "uranium" and the other is "God." After depicting these serious thoughts of Phil, the author makes Phil and Ed become bed fellows and have sex in Ed's flat. Ed has an iguana as his pet.

Vikram Seth describes the beginning of love between man and man as naturally and easily, without any hesitation, as between a man and a woman. Phil who was chaste for a year cannot control himself before Ed. At this juncture the author asks the readers, whether it is right, this should put the Muse to flight?

The delineation of Ed, unfolds the life style of rich, single men. Iguana is his strange pet, the apartment has a small pool for that animal. There is a photograph of Lana Turner, the famous Hollywood star. A Holbein sketch of Thomas More, a patron saint of Ed, is also there. Phil and Ed live together for three evenings and find perfect and happy companionship. Yet the author has presented Ed as having a conflict between sexual desire and religious doubts and a sense of guilt. Ed feels a sense of sin consciousness for his action, but cannot overcome his desire. Ed feels that he is sinning against Jesus, who sacrificed his life for the good of the people. He quotes the Bible: "If a man lie/ With a man, he must die?" "It is written in Leviticus, chapter 20/ Verse 13/" For him it is a temptation. He says his body is "God's instrument" (Chapter 4, sonnet 52). But all these arguments of Ed are only 'Bullshit' to Phil. He asks Ed: "But what was wrong or odd/ With last night's loveliness between us?/ . . . I'd say he blesses/ the innocent bodies that express/ so forthrightly, such happiness." Thus Phil not only defends gay relationship but justifies also. This fourth chapter has 53 sonnets and is filled with many serious discussions and romantic incidents.

Chapter V

The fifth chapter consisting of 44 sonnets continues the depiction of the relationship between Phil and Ed. Before beginning the episode of Ed and Phil, the author in four sonnets describes the reaction of an editor, when he hears that Vikram Seth was writing a novel in verse. The editor, publisher, a professor, a critic—all voice their doubts about the use of this device in writing a novel. In this context, Vikram Seth writes: "A winter is a mere arthritic/ Among these muscular Gods of Taste." Yet he prefers to write this novel only in verse.

Ed broods on the discussion he had with Phil on homosexuality and religion. He thinks he would never again hear from Phil. Ed goes out for a drive, watches the bright city at night. Lights shining on the water, bright Venus in the sky, the tall bridge and the Golden Gate Park enthrall him. He feels: "it is the loveliest city in the world." Yet his mind is sad. He returns home and thinks of writing to Phil, but prefers to visit personally. What does Ed find in Phil? The author writes "the very fact that Phil is married and living with his young son succeeds in giving/ Him the attraction in Ed's eyes/ of someone sound and worldly wise." But how far it is true is questionable. A month passes in uncertainty. There is no phone call from Phil, Ed decides to visit his sister Sue, takes the address of Phil's flat from her and visits Phil's flat with the iguana. He teaches chess to Paul and is very friendly with the child. After Paul sleeps, there is again a discussion about sex. Ed cannot shed his guilty feeling; neither can he shun the desire. Phil frankly says he likes Ed's body. When Ed is in Phil's flat Rowena comes, she is attracted by Ed. She behaves rater mischievously and provokingly with Ed. She "Pinches Ed's ass from friendly habit/ Ed, like a Schizophrenic rabbit/ Ekes out a terror stricken smile/ This shows how sensitive and shy Ed is with women. She invites Phil and Ed to attend olive picking. Phil cannot avoid it. Ed too has to go.

Before this olive picking, Phil has arranged for a grand breakfast, to which Sue also is invited. Ed is compelled to stay. Vikram Seth elaborately describes the breakfast. There are six kinds of cereals, wafer, syrup, sausage, jam, scrambled eggs, French toast, hot coffee. This sumptuous breakfast is organised by Mrs. Craven. Joan and Matt, the doctors, too attend the breakfast with their son Chuck. We should remember, at the end of the novel, Matt and Joan are dead in an accident and Chuck becomes an orphan. Perhaps this is the last time we see these friends happy together. Why is this celebration? What are they celebrating? Phil explains: "Oh yes—just that we are still alive, I guess." Phil's words sharply bring out the uncertainty of life, that too in the present-day world of Nuke wars, terrorism, radiations and many man-made and natural disasters. Unaware of the future, Phil's words seem to forecast a doom. This breakfast gives way to olive picking in olive groves. The process of olive picking and pickling picturise the pastoral activities and are foils to the mechanical urban activities. Mrs. Craven, like a matron, bosses over everybody, instructs, orders, demands every one to comply with her command. Drs. Matt and Joan are an ideal couple. Paul, Chuck and all others enjoy this olive picking as it is pure enjoyment on the lap of nature. Even the iguana and Ed enjoy the green olive grove and the bright sunshine, children playfully poke at him. Not used to this he is shocked and wants to come to the shelter of his master Ed. This makes Rowena laugh. She says, having such a robust body the iguana does not hurt the children. She says that iguana should be the symbol of friendship between the countries and people. Iguana being herbivorous cannot hurt eve a rabbit. After the olive picking and preparing sixteen jars of pickle, Ed decides to drive back "once more, once more back to the city/ To Monday's mundane nitty-gritty/ of nine to five." Phil asks him to stay another night and Ed obliges.

Chapter VI

In the sixth chapter, the story shifts to the fortunes of John and Liz. They are happy together, but small irritations, intolerances have started, Liz, being in the habit of taking excess sugar has to control and she has become diet conscience. She decides the upper limit of intake of sugar as three spoons daily. The diet restriction is too much to bear for her. She imagines she is suffering from the attacks of migraine, or she feels darkness is descending upon her eyes. John's playful comments enrage her. She threatens that she "shall boycott all food." She feels life is not charming without having freedom to indulge in such a sinless occupation as eating whatever one wants. The companionship of John and Liz continues, they think of getting into a new apartment to live together. After getting it they busy themselves in moulding it to their own taste and convenience, and necessity, like paints, polishes, mellower lamps etc. John is happy, enjoys morning coffee and newspaper. He now realises "In life's brief game to be a winner/ A man must have—oh above/ All else, of course, someone to love."

Here, the author interferes and says "Ah John, don't take it all granted/ Perhaps you think Liz loves you best/—A cuckoo's bomb lies in nest/ Be warned. Be warned—/ Now a cat enters the game." That villain cat Charlemagne is jealous of John, he hates John for John has usurped the realm of Liz's love, which was till then reserved only for Charlemagne. Sharing Liz's bed, and locking Charlemagne outside the door are criminal offences in view of Charlemagne. This cat is Liz's pet and her companion from her childhood days. He had followed her even to her school and college too like Mary's lamb. Vikram Seth describes effectively the role of Charlemagne in bringing estrangement between John and Liz. One night, when Liz is working late in her study, this vile cat urinates on the bed near the head of John. Basically John is not a cat lover, he bursts into her study naked, shouting that he will kill that hellish beast. With all his seriousness John cuts a very sorry and comic figure. But Liz questions him whether he had teased the cat. This further infuriates John. John and Liz exchange words. John is extremely annoyed. He locks his bedroom door, but Charlemagne is bent upon causing distress to John. He destroys John's custom-made pig-skin briefcase. John says, "today my briefcase is targetted, tomorrow he will gouge out my eyes." John says to Liz that he is scared of this Charlemagne. He demands, either she has to get that cat declawed, or he himself will saw them off. Once John had said "a wonderful cat" about this cat. Liz cannot imagine the cruelty of declawing a cat. She begins to weep, John consoles her. This matter is taken to Jane. She advises to take Charlemagne to a cat psychiatrist. The Charlemagne episode brings forth the extreme attachment of some people to their pets—at the cost of distress and discomfiture it causes to their human near and dear ones. We know of vets treating all physical ailments of animals. Now there should be psycho-clinics for animals also. So, the cat is sent to a psycho kitty, three times a week.

After this solution to Charlemagne's nuisance, the author takes us to Jane, her sculptures, her cats and her loneliness. John and Phil are too busy to meet Jane. Once Phil comes to meet John and Liz, mainly to clear some of his legal doubts with Liz. Phil and his friends participate in peace march demonstration against Nukes and the production of these weapons in labs. Difference of opinion arises about this issue between John and Phil. John thinks that the attack on lab is undemocratic. He accuses Phil that he and his friends are screwing the country, claiming to be the high priests of humanity. This part of the novel brings forth the political social issues like Peace Marches, curbing of media in U.S.S.R, K.G.B. etc. Phil opines: "Humankind/ Extends beyond our grim theocracies/ or constitutional plutocracies"/ He leaves some literature for John to read. John too sends a present, an abalone shell to Paul. Ed comes, Liz seems to be sad and meditating on something. The forty nine sonnets of this sixth chapter reveal the varying moods of Liz, different viewpoints of John and Phil, Charlemagne's intrusions in the happy lives of John and Liz.

Chapter VII

The seventh chapter consists of 48 sonnets, and acquires universality, owing to the problems it deals with and the picture it presents. The author directly takes us to the streets where the demonstrations are held and speeches are made. This chapter presents the intensely sophisticated, dangerous tensions of the contemporary world, especially the danger of radiation. The author uses bitter irony in describing the modern weapons and bombs. It is learnt that Phil takes part in this protest against weapons and the lung-less lab, where these weapons are produced and he is arrested. Liz who had come there with her cat makes a speech. Perhaps these incidents further help Liz and Phil to come together. The elaborate description of the protests in which citizens from all walks of life participate, is not limited only to America. The problems and dangers of Nukes, and radiation is a universal one. Thus this chapter acquires universal significance. There were placards on which these slogans are written. "I am my brother's keeper" [Cain had said "Am I the keeper of my brother?" Biblical allusion], "Work for life not death," "Strive with strife" etc. These placards are held by the handicaps on wheel chairs.

One can easily see the severe criticism of the American policy on nuclear weaponry. Though outwardly it is shown that America loves peace, it is shown here it is not so by the huge production of war weapons. As this chapter brings before us the present political and social scenario, it becomes a crucial one. In the first three sonnets of this chapter, Vikram Seth's general observations concerning our earth, fragile lives, and hate that envelops the earth are worth reading. He writes "The night of hate that covers earth/ the generous country of our birth/ The single lend from which we borrow/ All that is ours—air, insight, tears/ Our fragile lives for few years/ That night of hate grows dense around us/ We laugh through what we can't dispel/ While apathy and terror hound us/ On well-intentional path to hell." He questions "what after all is earth's creation?" "A virus in the morgue of space." These observations, the depiction of the demonstrations, gives a seriousness to the novel and elevates it to certain height from the evocation of mere superficial, mediocre, low-key life of modern man, and unfolds the noble and lofty thoughts that dwell inside him. These protestors are ready to risk prison to defy the weaponry. This assembly of protestors consists of young couples, school children, grandmothers, old hippies, punks with hair dyed green, staid suited men, all walk together "hand in hand" to the place "Where death is planned." It is the unanimous protest and effort of mankind to save itself from destruction. What about the people who devise these weapons? Can they be called scientists? Or manufacturers of death? Or in Russell's words only the merchants of death? The whole chapter provokes us to think about the sinister relationship between science and war weapons since time immemorial. The author writes that these folk who devise weapons don't think they plan death. But the most recent bomb [it was dubbed as "the cookie cutter"] batters live cells, but leaves buildings and machines intact." This butchering brain spawn is in fact soothingly styled a "radiation enhancement device by these men." Thus the satire and irony reach a climax in this depiction of modern researches, scientists and their new inventions. This reminds one of Albert Camus's words, that civilisation and progress means, to find a means "to kill as many people as speedily as possible." But now it is slow killing. Perhaps Vikram Seth has in mind the people still suffering with the effects of radiation in Hiroshima. He attacks the labs that produce and the people who use the bombs: "They breed their bombs here; others aim them."

Twenty sonnets are reserved for Father O' Hare's lecture. He is sixty years of age, slightly fat, wears spectacles, clad in an untidy black garment. With his deep and clear voice, with his deep knowledge of scriptures he impresses the gathering, the government waits to stop this movement and is ready with police and vehicles to arrest the activists. Though there was a huge gathering, peace prevails. O'Hare addresses people as friends, sisters and brothers, sons and daughters (Sonnet 16) (reminds one of Vivekananda's Chicago lecture). O'Hare advises to stop the growth of the week of hatred. He gives the example of the countries, where there was mutual hatred in the beginning and how this hatred turned into friendship gradually. He points out that Jesus was hanged because of hatred. O'Hare says that the church should interfere and prohibit the Government, from Nuclear Warfare, there should be a freezing of nuclear weapons. He observes that America has killed innumerable number of men of different races and communities. American Government, it seems has sped up wars. Through O'Hare, the author criticises the American military policy. After this speech of O'Hare, many people from the gathering express their opinions. Liz too is asked to make a speech. She asks not to destroy humanity and the ozone layer by making bombs. It was of utmost importance. At the same time environmental pollution should be avoided.

Chapter VIII

The meeting of Phil and Ed is narrated in this chapter. Ed comes to Phil's house. A discussion takes place between them. Phil asks Ed, about investing some days of his life for protesting, for simply by praying, the megatons of weapons will not melt. But Ed has his own views about this. Phil describes his experience of prison. The activists were put in a circus tent, for, the huge number of protestors could not be accommodated in the lungless country jail. They plan to have some coffee and go out. When they return home Phil asks Ed to share his bed. Ed refuses. An argument and a fight ensue. Ed does not yield to the pressure. Ed thinks it is against religion to indulge in homosexual. Phil tells Ed that the beliefs of religion change with time. But Ed cannot accept it. He says so and firmly believes that truth remains the same in every age. This discussion about religion between Ed and Phil, Ed's sunset guilt become the cause of their separation. Phil explains that this lovemaking between man and man is no sin, it is not the Middle Ages. He asks Ed: "what facet of our love outrages/ Your puritanical purity?/" But to Ed "The church's/ Teachings are much the same as when/ Christ came to save fellowmen." This time Ed does not agree to have sex with Phil. The eighth chapter consisting 37 sonnets ends with the separation of Phil and Ed.

Chapter IX

In the ninth chapter, the story returns to Charlemagne, psychokitty. The cat is not cured of his jealousy and hatred he felt towards John. The rift between John and Liz slowly widens because of this cat. Liz pleads for Charlemagne and says "He's brave, fine, and useful cat." John retorts "He'd be more useful if I canned him/ for rat food—though I doubt a rat could stand the stench." John blames Liz as a cat freak "You cat freaks are quite simply crazy/ you'd weep more tears for one lost pet. Than for a flood in Sulawesi/" John thinks, could he have known their intense attachment of Liz to her cat, when he first met her? Had he not said it was a wonderful cat? Now he is so upset that he wants to get out of the apartment for a while. He meets Phil outside the door, Phil inquires about Liz. John's reply surprises Phil. John is clenching and unclenching his fists. So Phil asks him what's vexing his mind. John answers "I've had a drenching in the cold spring of truth. . . . That more than me Liz loves that cat." Phil defends Liz, but John frowns and says that it is not only that horrible cat but his freedom to be alone, to watch football, eat junk food, all is gone now. He cannot read what books he buys, for, he is dragged off to some dumb ballet, feeble concert, or worse play. But still there is love between John and Liz. John still feels Liz is a "dynamite in bed." Yet a rift is opened between them. John asks about the injury and black marks Phil has got on his face. Phil tells he got these in a scuffle he had with Ed, and he reveals his relationship with Ed. This shocks John. He says Phil is a married man, and wonders what pleasure he can get with a man. John says once Ed was his roommate, if he had tried this on him, John would have knocked off Ed's head. By the time they return home Liz has come home. She asks Phil to come inside. She cannot fathom the reason for the sternness and seriousness on their faces. When she asks, Phil casually speaks the truth that the affair between Ed and himself has greatly upset John. John becomes terribly angry when Phil shamelessly announces this to Liz. When Liz asks John to be cool and "it's not that bad" etc. John shouts dumbfounded: "Ed is your brother! I'm astounded/ that you can get so cool when he/ And Phil . . . (he shudders helplessly)." John says "anything goes in this mad city." John further points out, Ed must either be sick or mad and accuses Liz that she too must be as bad, and even that gross cat too. He says it is a pity that Ed has not yet gone to a shrink (Psychiatrist); he suggests it to Phil too. Phil goes out, there is a row between John and Liz. However Liz comes out to pacify Phil, who had sat shaking in his car before the steering wheel. She is not making any efforts for a patch up between Phil and John. She says sorry and asks Phil to open the door. Liz says she had known this thing—the affair—a month ago. Phil wonders, "Did Ed convey this to you?" Liz says that on Sunday before the equinox Ed and Phil "wore the same mismatched socks." Phil says that they had thought they were very discreet. Then they go on a drive, they talk about the arrests made during the demonstration. When Phil was arrested, he had asked Liz to go to Paul and inform him and show a little care to him. Liz had taken two "tintins" to Paul, the boy felt happy. Phil thanks Liz for this. Liz says that the books Phil had left for John to read were read by her. They discuss John and Ed. Phil discloses to Liz Ed's conflicts between religious feelings and homosexual desire and his guilt feeling. Liz reveals that Ed thinks Phil as a hero. She expresses her present feelings towards John. They become uneasy, because of the intimate talks, but they begin to talk about Paul and the innocent pleasures of childhood. Their old ease is regained. This incident helps in the development of mutual understanding and intimacy between Phil and Liz and paves the way for further strong bonds in their lives.

Chapter X

The tenth chapter consists of 40 sonnets. It directly takes us to the clapboard church and its white steeple and to the thanksgiving services. This chapter presents a pleasant contrast with its pastoral atmosphere and the simple traditional living, farm activities. A gathering of happy people come out from the church. There is good sunshine, the harvest of vine is good. Mike Dorati, father of Liz, Ed and Sue is farming his vineyard for the last forty years. Mrs. Dorati is arthritic and worries about the marriages of her children. She feels happy that John is ready to marry Liz. Ed does not pay any heed to the words of his mother. Sue is about to get married to Art. With two prospective sons-in-law Mrs. Dorati feels happy. When Mike Dorati leaves home to Pete, the brother and sisters immerse themselves in happy conversation. They tease one another and indulge in past memories. Ed has brought his iguana. The cat is not looking at it. John too is not looking at Ed. Sue has won a scholarship and has decided to go to Paris. So they have decided to postpone the marriage. Mrs. Dorati feels unhappy, because she cannot see her grandchildren soon. Though John is watching the T.V., his mind broods upon his friend Phil. Liz has told him that the affair between Ed and Liz is ended. Yet, "Phil's salvos at High Nuclear tech/ And Liz's legal volunteering/ oppress his mind."

After breakfast next morning, Mr. Dorati asks John to join him in pruning the vines. Mr. Dorati calls his wife Mary also to accompany them and to help her to walk, gives his arm to her. Mrs. Dorati watches them working. John learns to clip and pure vine. After they return home from the vineyard, the members of the house group themselves, John and Liz walk hand in hand by the red water. John says that they should now think seriously about their relationship. It has been already a year since they first met. Moreover, Liz's people too are suggesting—he does not let out the word marriage. John is confident of Liz's approval. But Liz asks him to give her some time, this surprises John who fails to understand Liz's words.

Mr. and Mrs. Dorati present a picture of happy married life, with grown up children, a farm etc. If they are unhappy it is only about the children, not in their mutual relations. It is a perfect man-woman relationship. But that kind of happiness is not found in their children's lives. The texture of life is totally changed, this change and the generation gap are brought forth in these delineations. Mr. Dorati himself says to Liz, about her mother's increasing pain, she may not survive for long. Liz wants to have an intimate talk with her mother.

Ed returns home with mail and the whole story changes suddenly. Looking at the mail, John spots a thick letter addressed to Liz. He recognises the handwriting. It's Phil's letter. This letter shocks and pains him. When Liz comes there to go to the living room to see her mother, John suddenly grabs her shoulder and asks: "You plan to lead him on and cast him off/ With the same alacrity/ That has dropped Claire or you've dropped me." Actually Liz knows nothing about the contents of the letter. An argument ensues. Liz asks John, not to accuse her of having an affair with Phil. John repents, tries to clutch Liz's hand, but she shudders at the touch. Though the reconciliation of Liz with her mother becomes possible, her relation with John ends.

Chapter XI

Consisting 55 sonnets, the eleventh chapter depicts the surprising shift in the story. Instead of John, we see Phil as the bridegroom and Liz the bride. The scene presents the some clapboard church, the context "the bride and the groom have left to exchange a "private kiss" that "May sanctify their nuptial bliss." Through the dialogue of the sisters Judy and Juliet we come to know about the wedding of Phil and Liz. Phil's mother, old Mrs. Weiss, flown from Florida creates a scene. Mrs. Dorati is very happy about her daughter's marriage, she guides the guests towards the cake. The children Paul and Chuck are happily cutting the cake. Phil and Ed are a little embarrassed to meet each other. Yet Ed Jokes about Phil's black clothes and leaves. Liz wonders, whether she can behave normally with John, Jane has not attended the wedding. Liz assures her father that she will be happy with Phil as he is gentle.

After the depiction of these incidents, the author thinks these in a flashback (sonnet 14) and informs the reader what pushed Liz to marry Phil in such a haste. The author says, "her mother's illness, the traumatic parley with John, and Phil's long brief read, left Liz so, pale and erratic in thought, mood, look and word" that Ed, steps up to her as a "Psychiatric saviour." He offers her brandy, soothes her as a brother and asks whether she still loves John. Liz asks him about his relation with Phil. Ed answers their affair was ended. Then Liz explains how she had decided to marry Phil in such a hurry. Liz was the attorney from the defence, when Phil appeared before the judge in that trial regarding the protests (lung-less lab etc.), Father O'Hare was already sentenced on the previous Monday. The judge was thinking of sentencing the other five also, including Phil. But Liz with her vehement and eloquent arguments had saved them. After the courtroom celebrations, Liz had taken her clients to lunch. Phil congratulated Liz on her superb argument. But Phil discerned a sort of uneasiness and vexation on the face of Liz. He thought it must be something regarding John and asked whether something had upset her and was that about John. Liz answered it was all over and she would never marry John. All of a sudden Phil asked: "Oh well then, Liz try me instead." That was how they had decided to get married. There was mutual understanding and liking; moreover Paul too liked Liz. So they did not want to waste time. Thus the author writes, they, "two weeks later, man and wife/ Set sail on the calm pond of life."

What was the effect of Liz's decision on John? He tossed Liz's letter and invitation into the trash can, tearing the letter into fine strips, wrote a short note to Liz that he had received the letter, had destroyed it unread. A lawyer would meet her and clear the things if needed—regarding the flat key etc. John did not read the note sent by Phil. He would not understand or own that he "Helped generate this new equation." He thought that Phil and Liz had in reality caused a "breach of trust."

John becomes morose. His sadness and loneliness increase, but he cannot weep and find an outlet. He thinks of Janet, but as he has ignored her all these months, now he is ashamed to call her. Yet, Phil and Liz think of John and send him a new year gift, John returns that gift, an Italian alabaster dove. Liz again attempts rcconciliation: but her card "a single pleading line" arrives at Valentine and this seals the path of communication. John's life grows lonelier and more painful. He develops a sort of dislike towards life itself and begins to frequent "Mixed single bar" the "Winking Owl." The news of his visits to the Winking Owl spreads, Jane decides to meet him at the Winking Owl, but when she comes there John is not there. After sometime he comes, but does not talk with Jane warmly. However they meet again at Café Trieste, the old warmth is reawakened. The meetings in the week-ends increase. They realise their mutual love. Jane remembers the life of her grandmother, who journeyed to a foreign continent for her husband's sake. He died of a brain tumour in 43. She lived thirty years without any complaint. This episode of Jane's grandmother is another incident that reveals the change in the texture of life, that occurs along with the flow of time. In this eleventh chapter, the author tries to put some life again in John's life through Janet, who had once tried to bring happiness in his life by putting ads (Refer to the first chapter). The problem with John is that he cannot give himself completely to anything or to anybody. He cannot accept anybody wholly and completely with all their weaknesses and defects. Unless he learns to expand his self, include his near and dear completely inside that circumference of self, he cannot be happy.

Chapter XII

Chapter twelve contains 36 sonnets and depicts the renewal of the previous friendship between John and Janet. Though their working hours are different, they meet for a few hours in a week. Janet wants John to restore his friendship with Phil and Liz. But John has sealed the door of that friendship. Janet knows, what happened among these three can be a fit subject to a Shakespearean tragedy, yet she thinks that envy and hatred have no place in human life. John receives bonus and promotion, Janet and John enjoy the pleasant spring. Meanwhile Janet arranges for the exhibition of her sculptures, in a small gallery on June 10. Though the works are really good, there is adverse criticism. Janet is pained by this and weeps in private with frustration, at this universal condemnation. John consoles her saying, "Your time will come Jane, just you wait." Jane meets Liz, Phil and Paul at "Marcus." It is a pleasant meeting, Jane learns that Liz is in the family way, it is already the sixth month of the pregnancy. This gives the reader the correct span of time. Janet invites them to the party she has arranged on Friday night.

Jane's party in which she can never participate is an example of irony of fate. Jane is busy in arranging the party. John has taken the onus of looking after the guests. Jane's vehicle has carried her sculptures for years and now it has become old and rusty. In that vehicle Jane drives to Stanford to meet her friend Sue, who is leaving for France, she meets Sue, assists her in packing and with a heavy heart starts, for she has to be on time to her own party. But Jane's vehicle does not start. When she contacts Phil, he suggests her to contact Dr. Matt, who would be coming northward that day and Jane can try for a ride with Matti Joan and Chuck. So, it is arranged. John is busy in the party, worried about Jane being late, he is looking after the guests. John becomes anxious, angry and disappointed at Jane's delay in coming there.

When Phil and Liz too come to the party, John almost freezes. Along with these descriptions, Seth gives an account of a happy conversation among Matt, Joan, and Jane in the car. "Slowly dusk turns to dark" and Jane looks at the starts, etc. Phil wants to know whether Jane has met Matt. It is known that Matts have already left. John bursts "Damn, damn, that woman and her wiles" about Jane, yet he smiles. Even with Jane's absence the party is in full swing. The phone rings and abruptly everything ends. The author brings out this catastrophe so effectively, economically and so suddenly that it numbs the senses of the reader for a moment, not knowing clearly what has happened. John lifts the receiver: "Yes . . . Hayakava . . . what . . . police?" "All sounds around him swiftly cease/ Phil looks at John: eyes closed and gasping/ As if for iife and death, he stands/ The Micky Mouse phone in his hands/ Reiterating, without gasping/ Three words that gradually sink in/ As he repeats them, 'Next of kin?'" All other details are narrated in the final chapter of the novel, keeping the reader on tenterhooks, and plunging John in the pool of grief, agony and unbearable loss.

Chapter XIII

The unceasing cycle of birth and death and birth will go on for ever. The accident ends in the death of Janet Matt and Joan. Only Chuck has survived. The final chapter of the novel consists of 52 sonnets and the story is resumed after one month of Janet's death. Joan had flung herself across the body of Chuck, her son and had saved him. The driver of the other vehicle that collided with the car of Matt was only a high school boy. When he gained consciousness he had sobbed. The boy pended guilty and the trial ended. The judge suspended the licence of the boy for one year, for the judge felt: "The dead are dead, why destroy the youth of a boy."

Chuck stays with Liz and Phil. His broken arm is healing, but it is difficult for him to come to terms with the death of his parents. He always pleads to take him to his parents' home. Phil and Liz feel very sorry for Jane's death. Yet life has to go on. Another drummer joins the band 'Liquidsheep.' Meanwhile, after Janet's death, critics shower high praises on her sculptures. Rowena is elected to city hall as a councillor. Phil and Liz's family increases. Liz gives birth to a male baby, Liz's mother sees her grandchild and is happy. Liz and Phil name their child after John and want him to be the child's God father.

Liz's mother dies in the mid-harvest season, she no longer suffers the pain of cancer, only after her death it is known she was suffering from cancer. "Her ashes mingle/ With vineyard earth till not a single/ Mark of her signifies/ a spot where something of her lies" reveals what a leveller death is. Yet nature never ceases to bring spring on the golden birches the mocking birds sing lucidly, A soft sun shines, A blue jay perches, the whales move southwards. But Matt and Joan's garden is untended, wrinkling unplucked olives thrive, magnolias shed their vein bruised petals. John's yard is full of weeds, dust settles in his disordered room, symbolising his mind.

After the accident, John wants to see Jane in the hospital, she is in a coma, John wants to say something to Jane and to know something from her. But the hospital authorities do not allow him to see Jane, for he is not her "next to kin." Jane breathes her last, without seeing John and this causes a great grief in him. He badly wants to know whether Jane had loved him. He searches her papers but fails to know anything for sure. John finds a sand dollar in her drawer, and by touching that he gets solace even in his sorrow. He is haunted by her face, her eyes, her voice. He feels her presence, he thinks he hears her voice solacing and comforting him: "I am with you, John, you are not alone/ Trust me my friend: there is the phone/ it is not me you are obeying/ Pay what are your own heart's arrears/ Now clear your throat; and dry these tears." These are the last words of the novel. John believes he is listening to the spirit of Jane. He has to learn to "pay his heart's arrears." Is John hallucinating? Will he come out of his melancholy? It is left to the guess of the reader.

Beginning with John's melancholic mood, the novel ends in John's melancholy and completes a circle.

Theme of Loneliness in Vikram Seth's *The Golden Gate*

S. KRISHNA SARMA

It is a trite statement that a writer 're-presents' life experiences through using artifice and thus distances the represented life from the observed reality, so much so that the ancients charged the poets with falsehood, and Plato denied them a place in his Republic. As fictional form developed, the 'representation' was further distanced from reality, as the more serious thinkers believed. The fictionist himself was dissatisfied with the simple, straight narrative strategies employed by the 18th and 19th century novelists (of France and England in particular). Thereafter, every writer sought to express his experience through more and ever more complicated strategies—the French Naturalism, the "Stream of Consciousness technique" of Joyce, Woolf, Symbolism of writers like Wilson Harris, fictional biography of South African and Malaysian writers, and triple level narratives like those of Janet Frame, included.

Use of verse as a narrative mode is an attempt perhaps in one more direction to objectify experience further, or to come closer to reality. Verse narration is not new to literature, though. Not only did the early writers employ verse for all their narrative works, but also many long narratives, like *The Faerie Queene,* contained a story line. Romantics like Scott and Byron, Victorians like Tennyson and Browning, and many turn of the century poets (including Sri Aurobindo) narrated tales in the verse form. But when a novelist uses the verse form as a narrative mode, not for its own sake as in Romantic poetry, but as a deliberate strategy, the case becomes complicated. The writer is choosing the verse form, not because he is incapable of prose narration, but because he wants to double distance from the experience he is wishing to present. Even Shakespeare was rewriting some of his dramatic themes in the course of his *Sonnets,* trying to achieve a shifted perspective to look at the same experience (assuming, that is, that the *Sonnets* constitute a fictionalization of some of the themes we encounter in the plays). In a similar way, the novelist who uses verse as a narrative mode is trying to objectify the experience that is already objectified.

When Vikram Seth came to employ the sonnet form (neither Shakespearian not Miltonic, though), he was deliberately introducing a further distancing—at the third level, the first two being the fictionalizing of experience, and the verse mode of narration. The verse mode tends to draw attention away from the experience to expression. The reader of *The Golden Gate* could not have missed the frequent play on words, for the sake of rhyming, apart from the puns and the heavily ironical (tongue-in-the-cheek) attitude. This puts a question mark on the writer's approach to his characters and to the events. The attitude smacks of light-hearted comedy: nowhere does the writer appear to be taking things seriously. This could be one important symptom of detachment: it shows that the writer has achieved what he had set out to achieve, namely, a total objectification, distancing, to reach a stage of pure comic detachment.

When we pare away the artifice of the sonnet, and then the verse form itself with its highly evocative language, we are left with a certain naiveté in the tale, if not in the telling. Is it only a boy-meet-girl tale, a tale of the eternal triangle, a tale of love and betrayal, or a tale of the varieties of sex, or is it simply the tale of San Francisco, with the city as the hero (—the evocative atmosphere around the bay and the Golden Gate warranting the use of the verse form and poetic language, and maybe the title is therefore justified!) Underneath all these layers do we also encounter a note of something much more serious? The writer's 'tongue-in-the-cheek' approach—as I said above—does not greatly help us to recognize the seriousness. But in the narrative, we become conscious that almost all the characters are suffering from a sense of loneliness, and all of their activities are but a struggle to escape from that sense, and that this "loneliness within our souls" (20) is the central concern of the writer.

As a matter of fact, the narrative starts on this note. John is lonely. "Young, employed, healthy, ambitious, sound, solvent, self-made, self-possessed", yet he suffers from ennui: he feels life slipping away: he feels "lonely and lost, sans love, sans lover", as he laments in self-pity. He wanders into an ice-cream parlour, and finds all folks enjoying company. "It hurts that only he's alone" (6). A successful scientist, working in the Defence labs, a handsome man, unmarried, yet he could only turn to Phil Weiss, his Berkeley friend, Janet Hayakawa, a former lover, or to books for company!

When he could not contact Phil, he turns to Janet for help,—Janet, a sculptor in bronze and iron. She returns his call late at night, and with great concern, fixes a meeting for luncheon. Listening to his plight and plaints, she decides that he should immediately have a lover. When the colleagues at John's office or those he might meet at museums are dismissed as unpromising, she suggests advertising. He objects even for this. So, on her own, she sends out an ad for a friendly female, under 30, "impulsive, fit and fun." After short-listing the responses, John has a meeting with two ladies on two Saturdays, "to breach this fearsome solitude" (30). And they thoroughly disappoint him.

It is in response to the same ad that he meets Elisabeth Dorati, "friendly, female, 27", a practising lawyer, much sought after by her colleagues. A sort of intellectual, yet beautiful, she spends her weekends at her family's vineyard, talking to her dad—in his brief appearance, putting us very much in mind of Eliza's father, Mr. Bennett of *Pride and Prejudice.* She had refused to surrender to the insistence of fellow lawyers, for she could not exchange her loneliness with tedium of being a lawyer's wife ("0 loneliness—or else, 0 tedium!" [40]). Without expecting too much from the encounter, John and Liz meet, and immediately click so well that when Janet comes in to watch the meeting, she finds them "rapt in discussion" (43), and so she slips out quietly.

John and Liz like each other as persons, as lovers and as company. They are charmed. They go to concerts, theatres, ice-cream parlours, and they walk the beaches of the bay, staring at the lights together, and gradually they drift into a comfortable relationship, "despite the operatic dissonances of Charlemagne" (51), her pet cat.

Phil is also a scientist working in the nuclear labs like John but he had given up his job because of his new zest for peace. He had had an unequal marriage with Claire, belonging to a stiff-necked family—her mother had frowned at Phil's crude air. When Claire quit, even his mother blamed him for the split. He is burdened with caring for Paul, his six-year old son, as well as trying to fill up the void in his heart. He meets John and Liz at a music concert, where Liz's sister Sue was playing the cello. He is introduced to Liz, and invited to a house party. At the party he is bored by the female company; he meets Janet, an acquaintance from the Berkeley days (he and John had double-dated Claire and Janet in those days), and Sue whom he duly praises for her performance at the concert. Though drunk, he still defends to John his decision to quit the lucrative job. His exhortation about peace impresses Ed, Liz's brother, usually never at a loss for words (though talk. about nuclear bombs or God would freeze him out cold). In his drunken condition, Phil could look kindly at this "intense, athletic, silent" (84) Ed, and slide into an easy companionship. He is in no condition to drive home. So settling Paul with his friends for the night, he allows himself to be driven to Ed's place to share his bed. They slowly slip into sex, because Phil hadn't had it since Claire left a year ago. They spend the weekend together,—the Socratic Phil apparently being what the immature Ed needed. But the religious side of Ed suffers compunction and guilt consciousness the next day. He argues with Phil against the 'sin' they were committing. Phil, who could not believe that God would mind

My touch, your trembling, our caresses,
The loving smart in your clear eyes,
My hand ruffling your hair, our sighs (98)

is displeased and is bitter over the broken relationship. But chance throws them together into a stress-filled friendship again, at Rowena's olive picking.

Life for John had been smooth. He moves in with Liz, and they plan to invite all friends to a party. He comes to believe that he had won at "life's brief game" (129), because he had succeeded in having "someone to love." Perhaps the conclusion would prove too premature for, with creatures like Charlemagne around, who could guarantee a victory to the likes of John? The jealous cat wages a war of attrition against her rival to Liz's affections, by clawing his briefcase, tearing his office papers, urinating on his bed, etc. The lovers altercate over the cat, and the compromise that follows the fight is an uneasy one.

After the protest show staged by the Peace marchers at Lungless, where even Liz is persuaded to speak, Phil and Ed fight over their friendship that had turned sour: Phil fights for the rights of the body, and Ed for Conscience. In a black mood, they come to blows resulting in a black eye to Phil. They relent, and resume their debate on love. Phil insists that they should defer to what the heart says:

Why won't you
Defer to that strong love instead
Of spectral voices in your head? (189)

and that "Love's whole *I* Or else it's nothing" (190) If the 'love' between these two is floundering on the rock of religion and conscience, that between John and Liz is floundering on the rock of dissonance the cat is causing. To Liz the cat is a dear, harmless one,—his claws are only 'nails,' but to John he is an incarnation of devilry. His remonstrations against the cat only upset Liz the more: "I love you, but I just can't stand you" (193), she says. He comes to realize that "more than me—Liz loves that cat" (195). When he comes to learn from Phil that his contused eye was caused by a fight with his lover Ed, he is shocked and disgusted; "a dense veil of hate" descends between the two friends. He complains to Liz, hoping to shock her with the perverse relationship between Phil and Ed, but shocking him instead of being shocked, she pooh-poohs the whole thing as being quite common. She tries to patch the rift between the friends, but without success. Going out for a walk with Phil, she finds an unexpected, but exhilarating, kinship with him, in terms of their upbringing, their taste for Tintin comics, etc. Their walk on the beach of the bay results in a new understanding. She even pleads on behalf of Ed and asks Phil to be more patient and understanding. But what had affected Phil through the last one year was the utter loneliness:

> Christ, I'm so lonely
> God knows I only
> Want to . . . to live
> Without emptiness—to give
> A little love, to get a little. (209)

Elsewhere too are to be found the victims of loneliness. Liz's father, Mr. Dorati is worried over the loneliness that is looming on the horizon in the shape of his wife's cancer: he confesses his pain to Liz: "You don't realize it can get/ Lonely at times" (228). John visits them to help in the grape harvesting, and there he comes across a bulky envelope received in the name of Liz: he recognizes the handwriting: it is from Phil. He charges Liz with having an affair with Phil behind his back. Sore over Charlemagne's cantankerousness, he feels this is the last straw, and he walks out on her "self-damned, self-banished." Liz is traumatized by his unreasonable anger and insinuations. She had planned to defer her wedding by a couple of years, but in view of her mother's critical condition, she decides to marry Phil whom, as she assures her father, she likes because he is "gentle to me." Both of them had enough of love, and had found that "passion's a prelude to disaster" (244). They agree to be man and wife on the simple basis of friendship and gentle understanding. They set sail "on the calm pond of life" (245)

For John, the all too brief honeymoon with love and happiness is over. He rejects every friendly gesture and overture from Liz and Phil to befriend him. "Lonely, and injured in his pride" (247), he goes to seed and, in a newborn cynicism, begins to pick up "new chicks" every night to temporarily offset his loneliness. The news of his degeneracy reaches Janet finally. She is greatly concerned for his well being, despite the offhand way in which he had treated her in the past. She still had a soft comer for him. She intrudes, again, into his bohemian life, and draws him out of himself—they go walking on the beaches, watching the migrating whales when the weather was salubrious, and also when the weather proved discouraging. She makes a mighty effort to "drive him from his embittered brooding against the cosmos" (262). The meetings lead inevitably to sex. And both avoid mentioning the word 'love.' He begins to realize that she hadn't lost her feelings for him over these intervening years (since the time they were lovers), and she, knowing the elation in the present relationship, is unwilling to besmirch the "clean fabric of their trust" (268) with the dust of the past. And significantly, Jan's two cats, Cuff and Link, are not at all upset by the intruder: their purrs indicate that he is as welcome to the affections of their mistress as her sculptures.

Janet had been working against a deadline for the exhibition of her works when she re-entered John's life. But the show ends in disaster, thanks to the unfriendly critique of the Press. She keeps her disappointment and frustration to herself, and plans a party for friends. Running into Liz and Phil at the exhibition—Liz is now six months pregnant,—she invites them too to the party, and fondly hopes that some kind of softening of the strained relations between them could be affected.

As destiny (or irony) would have it, Janet's vehicle breaks down on the day of the party. Phil arranges with his friends, the Lamonts, to pick her up. John, filling in for the delayed Janet, is faced with the task of entertaining Liz and Phil among others, and is angry that Janis being deliberately 'elusive'—not knowing that she had been in a road accident and fighting for life at that moment. The nursing staff at the hospital are callous, and do not permit John to meet Janis because he is not "next of kin": he merely wanted to see her for a moment if only to say just one word: "I love you," perhaps?—but by the time they let him in, Jan is dead. Now John knows the searing "spirit-baffling pain" (286), and the recognition of his own love for her pierces his heart. "To forget her for a minute, for an hour/ To be without her, was a fate/ More painful than this pain" (288), he realizes. There is further irony in the same Press, which had slashed at her works mercilessly not too long ago, coming out with undiluted praise for them. And it is ironical too that John comes to recognize her value to him, and he is haunted by her eyes and her face, only after her death. It is ironical,—tragically so in the case of Janet,—that "she died alone, with no one near heft" (292). All along, she had fought single handed against the odds of life and the world of art. John could not give the sympathy or support she needed, though he made use of her on occasions. The note she had left for him in the early days of their renewed friendship, calling him for dinner and a play, now stood before his eyes as a mute testimony that she had loved him—loved him "undeludedly": she was too wary to spell it out, being "self-protectingly derisive of love" (293).

At last Liz's time comes and she gives birth to a baby boy, much to the delight of her mother, who seemed to have extended her life solely for this purpose: (she dies a week later). Liz and Phil decide to name the child 'John' as a final gesture of friendship and send a card to the 'sleazy' John, inviting him to be godfather for their child. He remembers Janet, and imagines what she would say on this occasion: "I'm with you, John. You're not alone." Encouraged by that reassurance, he gets ready to bury the hatchet and accept the proffered hand of friendship.

One could see the book as a novel about California maybe about San Francisco,—nay, even about the Golden Gate and the bay around. But it could also be seen as a social 'comedy' of manners, especially in California of 1980s. Could it also be seen as a dissertation on love? Perhaps it is a maze of all the three themes: it could safely be described as a 'manners' novel, presented against the backdrop of the nature, weather and atmosphere of the city and the bay. And, the main characters approach 'love' (a synonym for sex?) as a panacea for the ills that beset them. The one supreme ill that seems to effect them, as most of the moderns, is 'loneliness'—emptiness within—of one kind or another. The compromise solution Liz arrives at is determined by two factors: a feeling that she shares with Phil, that passion leads only to disaster, and secondly, the need to accommodate her dying mother's wish to see at least one of her children marry and give her a grandchild.

John, with whom the narrative starts and ends, may be taken (apart from the landscape, perhaps) as the central character. He has too much passion and is too volatile. As we see, he lacks depth and a sense of humour. He easily forgets his involvement with Janet during the Berkeley days and makes use of her for his purposes. He cannot see the funny side of Janet's ad, nor smile at the atrocities of Liz's cat, nor at the odd relationship between Phil and Ed: he needn't have been so horrified at it: he couldn't have been so innocent as not to have heard of homosexuality. One may call him self-centred. On the other side is Jan—Janet--Hayakawa, who had always been in love with him, apparently, while she herself had all through been in need of love and support to the same degree as John, if not more. But she had "built a fort against the ache" (260), like her grandmother. And she possessed a remarkable sense of humour: it is this that helped her to weather the rough and tough of life and of the art world. It is the same sense of humour that prompts her to run to John's aid at the beginning of the narrative, and after his break up with Liz. There is so much of poise and balance in her that she would not dig up the past and thus attract a curse on the newborn relationship with John. It is the same balance which helps her hide her tears of bitter frustration at the critical tirade of the Press over her works, and plan a party for her friends.

Is it poetic justice (if one wishes to feel sentimental) that she is killed? Is she too good for the likes of John? Or is she intended as a part of the process of growing up for John? Perhaps his redemption lies not with Janet but elsewhere: it may rather lie in the place where he had been so unreasonable and rude. Perhaps it is just that, admonished by the memory of the dead Janet, he should seek solace through a return to Liz and Phil. the two whom he had insulted so cruelly, and become godfather to young John Weiss.

Not caring to touch upon the grimmer side of the problem of loneliness, Vikram Seth appears to imply that kindness and understanding, and not sex, the so-called bodily love, would be an enduring solution for the existential problem besetting humanity. What Ed had proclaimed in metaphysical terms, that lovers need "to shed more than their clothes" (182), Liz was able to translate into her sober, but pleasure-filled married life. And, through Janet, the writer shows that the cure for loneliness is 'giving' and not taking or demanding. That perhaps is the 'golden gate' that bridges the emptiness among the individuals.

Work Cited

Vikram Seth, *The Golden Gate,* Faber & Faber, 1999.

The Narrative Technique in *The Golden Gate*

SAHANA DAS

Introduction

Set in contemporary American society, the plot of *The Golden Gate* deals with five people and their kaleidoscopic interaction. The characters have been depicted in so much detail that it is easy for the reader to get caught up in their private lives. For instance, the Los Angeles reviewer of the book, X.J. Kennedy, found himself caring less about the author's skill than he did about how the story develops.

It is not easy, however, to ignore this 'skill,' especially in view of the formal nature of the novel. While one usually associates novels with prose, this novel is entirely in verse. Moreover, the verse itself is in the highly formalized structure of a sonnet-sequence. Even the acknowledgement, dedication, and the list of contents are made up of a sonnet each.

The topic under discussion in this study has been prompted by this profusion of sonnets. Is it merely a literary gimmick? Or has Seth used this unusual narrative technique for an especially productive purpose, relevant to the contents of the novel.

Unfortunately, there is little material available on *The Golden Gate* by way of literary analysis. While there have been numerous published reviews of the novel, they do not offer significant critical insight. Papers on Seth, read by such eminent scholars as A.N. Kaul, have not yet been published.

Vikram Seth himself was not available for discussion as he was busy with his forthcoming novel at the time this chapter was being composed. Perforce, I've had to base the analysis of *The Golden Gate*'s narrative technique on my own study of the text.

Why sonnets? It is my contention that the most obvious consequence of its use is to prevent audience-empathy. When a narrative uses the language of everyday speech, the reader tends to forget the conscious, creating mind of the artist, and gets immersed in an illusion of reality. But when a narrative is rendered in rhyme (and in a rhyme-scheme as complex as that in *The Golden Gate*), the reader is forced to become aware of its fictional quality and of the artificial process of artistic creation.

On analysis, the text of *The Golden Gate* also reveals other distancing devices used to keep sentimentality at bay. The choice of sonnets as a medium of narration, therefore, harmonizes with other aspects of Seth's narrative technique for this novel. All told, it appears to discourage audience-empathy and creates a point of view that is objective, ironical and detached.

Such a point of view is grafted on to a tale that has most of the ingredients of melodrama: sentiment, romance, sex, death and violent emotions. Analysing this unusual juxtaposition of a detached audience-view on the one hand, and a melodramatic, emotional tale on the other, makes for an interesting study.

Narrative Voice

A novelist selects the angle of vision with great care so as to interpret and illuminate his material in the best possible way. As early as in 1921, Percy Lubbock said, "The whole intricate question of method, in the craft of fiction, I take to be governed by the question of the point of view—the question of the relation in which the narrator stands to the story."[1]

The reader's point of view, to a large extent, depends upon the choice of narrative voice. In 1804, Ann Laetitia Barbauld had made a classification of the narrative techniques used in the novels of her time. It is to Mrs. Barbauld's credit that subsequent critical views on narrative technique coincide with hers at so many points.

Writing a Biographical Account of Samuel Richardson, Barbauld had charted out three ways of telling a story. The commonest way is what she calls the narrative or epic manner of narration. This is the method of Fielding in *Tom Jones* and of Cervantes in *Don Quixote* and of a large majority of novels written to date.

In this method, the omniscient narrator speaks in the third person. He may follow one or many characters for short or long sections of the book. He emphasises what he thinks is interesting and comments on it if he wishes. The reader's view is often guided and sometimes controlled by this narrator.

The second method, according to Barbauld, is that of memoirs. Smollett in his *Roderick Random* and Goldsmith in his *Vicar of Wakefield* have adopted this mode. The third among her categories has since been antiquated. This is the epistolary method: letters exchanged among the characters of the novel. This method, a favourite with Richardson, had been used in novels like *Pamela, Clarissa*, etc.

The manner of the memoirs or the autobiographical method of narration has helped to produce a good many masterpieces: *Robinson Crusoe*, *Jane Eyre* and *Great Expectations*, are all first person narrations. As Lubbock puts it, "If the story-teller is in the story himself, the author is dramatised; his assertions gain in weight, for they are backed by the presence of the narrator in the pictured scene."[2]

But the advantage gained in veracity and immediacy is lost by criticism on aesthetic grounds. Writers as different from each other as Trollope and Henry James reject it. Trollope fears that the narrative "I" may be prone to either self-glorification or pretentious humility. James, on the other hand, finds unacceptable, what he calls, the "terrible fluidity of self-revelation."[3]

Such is the criticism levelled against the autobiographical method of narration. But the first-person is sometimes used in the 'epic' mode of narration as well. The vital difference is that while in the former the "I" belongs to a fictional persona, in the latter it is the author speaking in his own voice. *The Golden Gate* belongs to this latter mode of narration.

The narrative style of *The Golden Gate* makes it clear to the reader that the narrator who stands apart from all the characters and writes about them in the third person is the author himself. He never lets the reader forget that it is he and he alone who is telling the story.

The point of view of this novel is like a camera which, at times, focuses sharply on individual characters: their private thoughts and feelings. At other instances, it pans a panoramic scene, describing, for example, a group of pacifists demonstrating in front of a nuclear armament-centre. Throughout, the reader sees it from the narrator's viewpoint.

Should the author speak in his own voice? E.M. Forster strongly advises against it. Dismissing it as mere "bar-parlour chattiness," he finds authorial intrusion most damaging to the novels. "Intimacy is gained but at the expense of illusion and nobility,"[4] he feels.

Disliking Fielding's proneness to address his readers directly, Walter Scott says: "These appeals to the reader's judgment, admirable as they are, have sometimes the fault of being diffuse, and always to the great disadvantage, that they remind us we are pursuing a work of fiction; and that the beings with whom we have been conversant during the perusal, are but a sort of evanescent phantoms, conjured up by a magician for our amusement."[5]

The major objection to authorial intrusion seems, therefore, to lie in the fact that it dispels the illusion of reality. In the following argument I hope to show that preventing this illusion is a very deliberate effort in the narrative of *The Golden Gate*.

Distancing Devices

In a manner that is almost Brechtian, Seth keeps alive the distance between the reader and his novel. Illusion of reality is dispelled at the word "go" as Seth opens his novel in the tradition of a fairy tale: "Once upon a time."

The medium of narration maintains this distance, as the words of the novel arrange themselves in a sonnet-sequence.

This sequence is quite unlike its literary predecessors and has a flavour uniquely its own.

As a form, the sonnet-sequence is as old as the fifteenth century. But, unlike the typical Petrarchan mode, *The Golden Gate* does not lack narrative cohesion. The plot is tightly knit. As the *Atlantic* reviewer of the book puts it, "The author is not tempted to windy divagations, and the reader is not tempted to skip."[6]

The common theme of most sonnet-sequences is that of love. In the Elizabethan and the Petrarchan sonnet-sequence. This love is depicted in the courtly tradition: the mistress is beautiful. Chaste, and unattainable; the lover/poet anguished by his unrequited love. Platonic love is celebrated and sexuality, though recognised, is played down.

The Golden Gate is also about love. But the definition of love here is very different. Chastity and availability of the mistress is not the issue at all. Consummation of love was the glorious conclusion towards which the earlier sonnets had moved. Here, physical consummation is the point of departure for the main issues in *The Golden Gate*.

Another vital difference between *The Golden Gate* and the sonnet-sequence of the past is that the modern novel does not talk of man-woman relationship alone. One of the most sensitively portrayed relationships in the novel is a homosexual one.

In choosing to write his novel in a sonnet-sequence, Seth is perhaps doing what T.S. Eliot did: alluding to another literary work or tradition for ironic purposes. The earliest sonnet-sequences exalted platonic love and in the dichotomy between the body and the soul, the latter always emerged the winner. The reader, with such an expectation of sonnet-sequences is thereby shocked into alertness, when confronted by this novel.

The sonnets of *The Golden Gate* are unlike the Petrarchan ones in that they are not in the quatrain-sestet form. As in the Elizabethan sonnets, the sonnets of this novel too end in couplets. Typically, the concluding couplet is pivotal to the Elizabethan sonnets. This is not true of the sonnets of *The Golden Gate*, where sometimes the sequence does not conclude with the sonnet. Mostly, however, the novel's sonnets function as structural units, marking one small step ahead in the narration. These sonnets end with a conclusive punctuation mark: a period, colon, question or an exclamation mark.

Seth has composed his sonnets in tetrameter lines. This in itself is remarkable as Seth rejects the more usual pentameter lines. The author refers to this choice rather flippantly:

> Why, asks a friend, attempt tetrameter
> Because it once was noble, yet
> Capers before the proud pentameter,
> Tyrant of English. I regret
> To see this marvellous swift meter
> Demean its heritage, and peter
> Into mere Hudubrastic tricks,
> Unapostolic knacks and knicks. (5.4)

The rhyme sequence is complicated—ababccddeffegg. Notwithstanding the difficulty of rhyming in the English language, this pattern is adhered to without exception throughout the novel. As may be noted, this rhyme-pattern results in the formation of three internal couplets (cc dd ff) in addition to the fourth, concluding couplet. Because of the profusion of couplets within each succeeding sonnet, a rhythm is set up which focuses attention away from the story, and on the text itself.

This effect of objectivity of the reader's perception is reinforced by other aspects of Seth's narrative technique. If the complex rhyme-scheme keeps the reader's point of view detached, the narrative mood, created by the novel's manner of narration, cancels all illusion of reality.

As mentioned in the previous chapter, there is abundant use of the authorial "I." Interspersed in the main line of the story, are direct addresses to the reader: "Dear Reader," "Gentle Reader," etc. Seth shares with the reader the process of writing his novel: the planning, the choice of narrative technique, censorship. At one point, he even pleads, "Dear Reader/ In mitigation, let me plead a/ Drainage of brain." (11.14)

There are also many autobiographical moments in the text where Seth mentions friends or discussions he has had in the process of writing this novel. A notable example is:

An editor—at a plush party
(Well-wined,—provisioned, speechy, hearty)
Hosted by (long live!) Thomas Cook
Where my Tibetan travel book
Was honoured—seized my arm: "Dear fellow,
What's your next work?" "A novel . . ." "Great!
We hope that you, dear Mr. Seth—"
." . . In Verse," I added. He turned yellow,
"How marvellously quaint," he said,
And subsequently cut me dead. (5.1)

These autobiographical pieces link the main text with the sonnets under 'Acknowledgements' and the 'Dedication.' In all these sonnets Seth speaks in his own voice, outside the plot in the novel; the sonnets being written in the same tongue-in-cheek mood. Together, they contribute to our sense not only that this is fiction but also that, after all, this novel is more a game than a sombre, psychological study of man in modern American society.

The most devastating distancing device in *The Golden Gate* is the novel's humour. The pervading light-heartedness along with the tongue-in-cheek manner which surfaces often enough, effectively breaks the charming but stupefying illusion of reality. For instance, consider the following sonnet:

Who was it said, "Love is the friction
Of two skins"? From "your place or mine?"
There follow weeks of sweet addiction
To insular if sparkling wine.
Liz, now addressed by John as "honey"
Responds to him with "funny bunny."
There diction has, alas, become
Incomprehensible and numb.

Their brains appear to be dissolving
To sugary sludge as they caress.
In lieu of fire, force and finesse,
We have a ballet now involving
A pretty pas de deux instead
With common Walkmans on their head. (2.56)

This sonnet describes a relationship which, besides forming the point of departure for the rest of the novel, in itself proves also to be intensely passionate. Yet, by presenting it in this fashion, any mushiness or excessive sentimentality is removed from it. The reader too finds that while he sympathizes with these individuals, he cannot empathise with them. Laughter has introduced an objectivity in response, that cannot be dispelled even by the most intense interest in the fate of the protagonists.

The Plot and Point of View

To maintain an ironic perspective, then, seems to be a sustained authorial effort through the novel. This objectivity of reader-perspective partners the plot of *The Golden Gate* in three different ways.

First, and the most obvious, is that it enables the reader to judge each protagonist impartially. The reader also gets a critical overall view of the situation charted out in the plot. This is the most common effect of the ironic point of view, used by novelists as diverse as Jane Austen and Hemingway.

The second way in which the reader's point of view gels with the contents of *The Golden Gate* is less common. I'd like to suggest that the detachment in the reader's perspective parallels the fear of emotional commitment in each of the five protagonists in the novel. Beyond a point, each would like to retain his/her identity and therefore shuns an emotional take-over by another individual.[9]

An analysis of the plot will illustrate the argument contained in the preceding two paragraphs.

The background against which the novel's plot is set is definitely recognisable as modern day America (timed clearly in

1980). This is a world of advertisements and consumer items which have little to do with human emotions. Sonnet 7 of the opening chapter has John amidst his favourite Pumpkin Pie and Bubble Gum flavours of ice cream. Yet, when he sees the various people sitting around in the parlour, "It hurts that only he's alone."

This dichotomy between private emotions and external milieu is even more acute in Chapter V, Sonnet 6 when Ed has had his first disagreement with Phil. His sadness is to be countered by the best "media strategy." The choice—between available brands ("Encore or Savor")—seems quite unrelated to the essential product, i.e., coffee. The sheer absurdity of the situation underscores its impossibility: after all, one cannot fight an emotional crisis with a cup of coffee, no matter what its brand name!

Minor characters, mentioned in passing as it were, play an important part in the creation of this modern social milieu. Figures like Tim Tarvesh and Professor Praft epitomise the futility of the conventional trappings of success, be it financial or academic. The comedy of Professor Pratt's constant harping on Pittsburgh (four books on the same idea and a few more in the making) indicates the trap one could get caught in.

Given the initial glamour and fame, the question arises: What next? Tim Tarvesh and Professor Pratt seem to be caught in a trap of their own making. Incapable of transcendent vision, blissfully unaware as they seem of their situation, their life is tragically futile. It is futile because it is stagnant and tragic because their habit of comfortable success has grown to be self-defeating and destructive.

The periodic appearance of these two individuals at strategic points in the novel is a sinister, and therefore frightening, reminder of what could happen to any intelligent, ambitious person hoping to succeed in conventional modern society. Phil, in giving up a lucrative career, seems to have tried avoiding this very fate.

The lives of five people are charted out against this backdrop: those of John, Liz, Phil, Ed and Jan. Each character knows, or gets to know, the rest at the very beginning of the novel. Each of them is defined within the parameters of profession, personal ethics, eccentricities and family and social connections. Family connections are described through information for John and Jan. in the case of Phil, Ed and Liz, there is actual depiction of the people involved: parents, offspring, neighbours and siblings.

A pervading theme in the novel is that of romantic love. It is presented as a possible weapon in the battle against the loneliness of life. Sensing that "his life has run to seed" (1.4), John looks for a companion to love and be loved by. Implicitly or explicitly, it is true for each protagonist that "to be a winner/ A man must have . . . oh yes, above/ All else, of course, someone to love" (6.13).

Of course, the definition of this romantic love is very conventional: passionate, exciting, and with the possibility of perfect communication between the lovers. Initially, the relationship between John and Liz is marked by almost incessant talk. It seems as though the sluice-gates of emotion have opened out. The resulting flood breaks resistance to communication and they prefer to "forgo/ The cinema for conversation" (2.49).

Phil's name connotes 'love.' He is the least conventional of the characters, with an open, non-conservative mind both in his vocation and in his love-relationships. Since his marriage with Claire has failed, he does not shrink from Ed's offer of homosexual love.

Noteworthy here is the author's effort to present this relationship in a sympathetic light. This effort doesn't appear necessary in the John-Liz relationship. Perhaps there are two aspects to understanding Seth's treatment of homosexual love in *The Golden Gate:* (a) the author's attitude towards such a relationship *per se*, and (b) homosexuality in the context of this novel.

Throughout, it is clear to the reader that the Phil-Ed relationship has all the love, warmth and sharing that usually characterises the best man-woman relationship. Even through the rather flippant and tongue-in-cheek reference to censors, the reader can feel the purity and almost elevated quality of their relationship. Set against such an atmosphere, Ed's withdrawal and guilt serve to run reader sympathy against him. It is Phil who emerges as a more natural and spontaneous person. It could be that Seth's Western upbringing, and the years spent in the U.S.A. (where homosexuality in this sympathetic light. Be that as it may, an analysis of Seth's possible stand on homosexual love per se is not ultimately relevant to this argument. More important from my point of view, is to study the part that homosexuality plays in this novel.

No matter what the society (i.e., whether Western or Oriental), tradition and conventionality frown upon homosexuality. I would like to suggest that Seth, in presenting homosexual love in a positive light, meets head-on the rigidity of conventional society. First he shows the beauty of the relationship shared between Phil and Ed. Then, by making it unsuccessful, he underscores the barrenness of society which now appears to be only superficially modern.

The modern cause of the breakdown of the Phil-Ed relationship is Ed's tortuous sense of guilt, justified by him in terms of conventional, religious morality:

> The point is that my body is
> Not mine alone—I don't disdain it—
> But it's God's instrument—my bliss
> Is in his will—and its perfection
> Resides in love whose chief projection
> Is to give life. All other use
> Falls short of this. It is abuse
> Even if lovers feel they're loving. (4.52)

I feel that it is extremely significant that Ed's guilt should be allied to religion itself is a product of 'civilised' society. Ed's sense of wrong-doing throughout his relationship with Phil is pin-pointed as a sense of sin. It is interesting that Ed's religion is not a personal, individualised religion. His religious leanings are along extremely conventional lines, equating religion with the Bible:

> The Bible says, if a man lie
> With a man, he must surely die (4.50)

From the above argument, we can see how religion becomes an emblem of civilised society and bears the onus of the breakdown of the love shared between Phil and Ed. Yet another (and more obvious) emblem of civilisation—the car—becomes instrumental in breaking up the happy family, causing also the death of Jan.

The Phil-Ed relationship is not the only one that fails in the novel. John and Jan had broken their affair before the novel begins, and the reader witnesses the breakdown of the John-Liz relationship.

Phil's reaction to Ed's iguana parallels John's dislike of Liz's cat. This distaste for the partner's pet starts as a joke but eventually becomes an important factor in the final break-up of each relationship. John and Phil's distaste of their respective partner's pets seems symptomatic of an intolerance on their part. On the other hand, the equally insistent need in Liz and Ed to cling on to the pet seems symptomatic of a fear of letting go of personal eccentricities, eccentricities which helped to identify them.

It is this intolerance and fear of a possible emotional takeover by another person that finally breaks each relationship and results in each protagonist rejecting romantic love. Liz, in fact defines love as "a tightening tether,/ A habit-forming drug" (11.13). She seems to echo the feelings of all the protagonists in the novel when she tells Phil: "I too don't feel sure/ I cannot trust passion any more: (11.22).

Liz, then, opts to marry Phil, while John (a little later in the novel) seeks peaceful companionship with Jan. These new relationship are marked by ease and lack of pre-conceived expectation, having none of the raptures of the earlier experiences. Liz's reason for choosing to marry Phil ("A good kind man who makes me laugh") results in a solid companionship with none of the trauma of romantic love. Theirs is a choice on the side of safety rather than excitement.

The reader is closely involved in the unfolding of the tale as summarised here. Nonetheless, the reader's response is skilfully manipulated. "Part of the novelist's art is to mediate between his characters and the readers; and he does so with every word he puts on paper, for every word he chooses furthers his expression of his attitude toward his characters and the total situation he is rendering," writes Walter Allen.[7]

Seth's manner of presenting this human drama is such that the reader can never quite sympathise with any one completely. The rejection or fear of love and emotional commitment shown in the text is, obviously, not an inevitable consequence of modern American life.

All the characters are subject to the reader's ironic scrutiny. As such, their deficiencies are never absolved by interpreting them as natural to the kind of world in which they are born.

For instance, the opening chapter introduces John as a product of modern conservatism, leading a superficially successful life. In close juxtaposition to the description of the artificiality of John's life are lines which describe the natural beauty available all around him. In Chapter 1, sonnet 2, John deliberately turns his mind to thoughts of electronic devices. Yet the awareness of silhouetted birds that "move cawing/ Across the pine serrated sky" serves to emphasize the sterility of his life. It is precisely because there are alternatives present that he recognises the emptiness of his life and "cries for help."

Reader-empathy is deliberately discouraged by the author even in moments of intense emotionality. When Liz married Phil, John's agony is narrated with vividity and sensitivity. There certainly is sympathy (both in the author's presentation as well as the reader's perception) for John in the face of genuine human suffering. Yet the support for John is far from being unqualified.

Reader-sympathy is controlled, even curtailed, by a critical insight into John's psyche:

> Lost in a savage transportation
> Of grievance, he won't own that he
> Helped generate this new equation
> Selective sensitivity
> To his ills, blindness to their feelings
> Of equal injury, his dealings
> With Phil and Liz to him seem just
> Reprisal for their breach of trust (11.27)

Even Phil, who appears to have most of the author's sympathy, does not escape such ironic undercutting. In a different way, he too is a stereotype: an 'intellectual' who makes a virtue of being unconventional. He is the type that attracts people like Rowena who finds Phil "ultra cool" (3.23).

In the face of Phil's militant unconventionality it is ironic that he has to take on a part-time job to meet the demands of his growing family. This is his truce with the very society he has so aggressively shunned earlier. The compromise is comic, and the comedy is directed against Phil.

Although the point of view is kept detached and ironical, the reader focuses on a tale that is surprisingly intimate, intense and emotional. There is thus a qualitative opposition between the reader's point of view and the tale itself. This very opposition is used to the greatest advantage in *The Golden Gate*. Herein lies the third function of the unique narrative technique of the novel.

Talking of the advantage of using the omniscient narrator Marjorie Boulton says, "he can show us some plan, plot or problem and let us watch with excitement as the other characters move towards it. Again, we can enjoy the ridiculous rather more when we are not invited to identify too closely with one character."[8]

This is true as long as the subject under scrutiny merits criticism. But sometimes, in *The Golden Gate*, the reader is confronted with issues of such worldwide relevance, that detachment from such issues is itself criticised. The reader is suddenly made to feel guilty for having an ironic objectivity that keeps a distance from things which demand a passionate involvement.

The issue of nuclear warfare surfaces time and again in the novel. The active stand that Phil takes against Lungless Lab serves to pre-empt his break with John. It also provides the occasion for Liz and Phil to get close to one another. Yet the length at which Seth dwells upon the issue seems to imply that its importance is more than its contextual one.

Father O'Hare's speech (Chapter 7, Sonnet 16 onwards) is written with a passionate sincerity which goes beyond just the particular occasion in this particular novel. It can perhaps be related to the author's personal ideology. The reader feels faulted in maintaining an objective distance when the issue in the text is as important as this.

With complete absence of glib complacency, Seth seems to be describing two levels of consciousness with regard to nuclear disarmament. On the one hand there are those incapable of looking beyond the here and now. These have the "it's just a job, for heaven's sake" (7.7) kind of an attitude. On the other hand there are the ones who see the ghastly implications of what is being manufactured in the Lungless Lab vis-à-vis Mankind and the entire earth.

The first type is projected, not so much as consciously exercising evil, but rather as ignorant people with limited awareness and perception. The author's sympathy is obviously with the second type, while the reader unwillingly finds himself aligned to the first.

It has been previously mentioned in this argument that symbols of 'civilization'—the car and the Bible—play a part in the destruction of romantic love. The world within the novel is linked to the reader's own world outside and the reader finds himself a part of all that he was so smugly and objectively criticising. Consider the following sonnet:

Dark night and silent, calm and lovely,

That stills the efforts of our lives,
Rare, excellent—kind, and behovely . . .
No matter how the poet strives
To weave with epithets and clauses
Your soundless web, he falters, pauses,
And your enchantment slips between
His hands, as if it's never been.
Of all times most imbued with beauty,
You lend us by your spell relief
From ineradicable grief
(If for a spell), and pain, and duty.
We sleep, and nightly are made whole
In all our fretted mind and soul. (5.39)

Here there is an unusual and sudden elevation, both in subject matter as well as in style. It is as though the author was indicating a context that is larger than and, at the same time, more mysteriously glorious than the immediate human context. It is at such poetic moments that the novel enlarges and transcends petty, personal concerns.

Discussing the novel as a literary genre, Lionel Trilling suggests that its greatness and practical usefulness lies in the unremitting work of involving the reader himself in the moral life. In *The Golden Gate*, the reader is suddenly shaken out of complacency in the face of a "diversified assortment/ Of persons wedded to the cause" (7. 41) of abolishing nuclear warfare. Here is an issue that demands personal commitment.

Periodically in the novel, there are moments of poetic transcendence. At these elevated moments, the narrative voice is divorced from, and lifted above, the reader. Objective detachment is itself undercut. The focus, in camera, does a volte face as it were, and the point of view of the reader turns inward, towards his own self, rather than outward on the narrated tale. The point of view of the reader, put to such a use, is perhaps unique to *The Golden Gate*.

Conclusion

In the introductory chapter, two questions had been asked: Why use sonnets as the medium of narration? And Are authorial intrusions justified? As far as *The Golden Gate* is concerned, the two are, really, related. The use of sonnets and direct authorial addresses to the reader, together create a reading atmosphere where the reader is always aware that this is fiction.

The novel is like a tale in the oral tradition wherein the listeners are acutely involved in the story and at the same time aware that it is not for real. Seth sets out to tell a story, a story that is intimate, emotional and passionate. Yet, with the help of various distancing devices, the reader is kept aware of its fictional quality.

This technique has a dual advantage. It retains the reader's interest and sympathy; yet maintains sufficient objective correlative for analysis and a non-sentimental understanding of the author's material.

In addition, the objective detachment on the reader's part is itself used to bring the reader closer to the novel: detachment is seen as undesirable. An accusing finger is pointed at all those who fear commitment. The reader himself is made to feel guilty for having an ironic vision that kept him at a distance from human contact.

Discussing George Eliot's dramatic use of the author's voice, Barbara Hardy says: "The narrative medium is composed of many voices. There is the direct speech of the author's pity, both for her own creatures and extending in generalisation to lament and admiration for all humanity. There is the more detached voice of irony and analysis. There is the omniscient warning, veiled and unveiled, working in the interests of aesthetic unity and dramatic irony."[9]

This is equally true of Seth's technique in *The Golden Gate*. Successfully combining the paradoxical qualities of sympathy and ironic perception, the novel carries an implicit warning: it warns the reader against having the sort of attitude that, for instance, Eliot's Hollowmen represent. Having courage of one's conviction is the only hope, both in private as well as public life.

NOTES

1. Percy Lubbock, *The Craft of Fiction* (London: Jonathan Cape, 1921, rpt. 1965), p. 251.
2. Lubbock, p. 251.
3. Henry James, Preface to *The Ambassadors* (1903), Qtd. Miriam Allott, *Novelists on the Novel* (London: Routledge and Kegan Paul, 1959), p. 261.
4. E.M. Forster, *Aspects of the Novel* (Cambridge: Edward Arnold, 1974), p. 57.
5. Walter Scott, 'Tobias Smollett,' *Lives of the Novelists* (1827). Qtd. Allott, ibid. pp. 269-70.
6. Vikram Seth, *The Golden Gate* (New York: Vintage Books, 1987), back cover.
7. Walter Allen, *The English Novel* (Middlesex: Penguin, 1954), p.16.
8. Marjorie Boulton, *The Anatomy of the Novel* (London: Routledge and Kegan Paul, 1959), p. 38.
9. Barbara Hardy, *The Novels of George Eliot* (London: Athlone Press, 1959, revised edition 1963), p. 177.

Bibliography

Bergonzi, Bernard, *The Situation of the Novel* (London: Macmillan, 1970).

Cowley, Malcom, ed. *Writers at Work* (London: Secker & Warburg, 1958)

Halperin, John, ed. *The Theory of the Novel: New Essays* (London: Oxford University Press, 1974).

Hazell, Stephen, ed. *The English Novel: Developments in Criticism since Henry James* (London: Macmillan Press, 1978).

Hardy, Barbara, *The Appropriate Form: An Essay on the Novel* (London: Athlone Press, 1971)

Karl, Frederick R., *A Reader's Guide to the Development of the English Novel in the Eighteenth Century* (London: Thames & Hudson, 1975)

The Golden Gate Discussed Stylistically While Seth Writes More Novels

M.A. YADUGIRI and GEETHA BHASKER

The Golden Gate[1] by Vikram Seth, being a verse novel, combines two literary forms, a sonnet sequence and a novel. It has been described as a realistic novel by reviewers and critics who have noted the truthful picture of the lives, loves and trials of California Yuppies in the eighties presented in 590 sonnets with the rhyme scheme a-b-a-b-c-c-d-de-f-f-e-g-g. In terms of function, however, it is better considered under fiction rather than poetry.

This article attempts to examine *The Golden Gate* as fiction (in verse) and to describe some of the important stylistic features that are used by Seth in the telling of the story. The focus is on three features that are crucial in any study of narrative fiction from a discoursal viewpoint, namely, the type of narrator/author-reader relationship that is projected in the text, the type of relationship between the reader and the fictional world that is created, and the perspective from which the fictional world in the story is presented.

One of the most significant devices found in narrative discourse is the type of narrator/author-reader relationship that is projected or the kind of voice that is heard in the telling of the story. There has been a long literary tradition of the use of an I-figure in novels and as Fowler (1977:83) says there are different kinds of I-figures found in novels both traditional and modern. In *The Golden Gate* too we find an I-figure who is not a participant in the events narrated but who tries to build a close relationship with the reader performing multiple functions.

First there are the instances where the reader is directly addressed. Seth uses this device for what Thornborrow and Wareing (1998:178) call "self-referentiality" to draw attention to the text itself. Thus we have in the beginning

> To make a start more swift than weighty,
> Hail Muse. Dear Reader, once upon
> A time, say, circa 1980,
> There lived a man. His name was John.

We find further instances of direct address to the reader whenever the narrator wishes to signal how the focus of narration will change or to indicate how the story will develop. Towards the end of chapter 2, commenting on John and Liz, the narrator begins sonnet 55 with

> The loving pair has bit the apple
> Of mortal knowledge. As we see
> The rosy half-light of love's chapel
> Halo their ardent heads, should we
> Hymn them in accents hushed and holy?
> Forbear, O Gentle Reader. . . .

Then in sonnet 57, the narrator signals the direction the text will proceed in.

> Come,
> Let's leave them here, the blessed yuppies,
> As happy as a pair of puppies, . . .

The sonnet concludes with

> but what transpires next
> Is furnished later in this text.

Following immediately is the first sonnet of chapter 3 which begins with

> As Liz and John move out of focus
> Into an amorous mist, let's shift
> Our lens, Dear Reader, to a locus
> An hour south along that rift

That unnerves half of California:

And in 3.2 we meet the other important character in the story, Phil and his son, Paul. The next direct address to the reader is in 4.34, where the narrator attempts to account for the 'authorial abstinence' that he shows.

Now, just as things were getting tenser,
And Ed and Phil were making love,
The imperial official censor
—Officious and imperious—drove
His undiscriminating panzer
Straight through the middle of my stanza.
Now, Gentle Reader, is it right
This swine should put my Muse to flight, . . .
Forgive me, Reader, if I'm surly
At having to replace the bliss
I'd hoped I could portray, with this.

The most striking instance of the author's attempts to take the reader fully into confidence so that all doubts regarding the verse form used for the telling of the story are set to rest occurs in 5.1 to 5.5. This has been widely commented upon by reviewers and critics too. The first four sonnets of Chapter 5 present a detailed examination of the various questions in the minds of others and the author himself regarding the form and an attempt to explain its choice. Sonnet 5.5 says

Reader, enough of this apology,
But spare me if I think it best,
Before I tether my monology,
To stake a stanza to suggest
You spend some unfilled day of leisure
By that original spring of pleasure: . . .
Eugene Onegin—like champagne
Its effervescence stirs my brain.

In chapter 11 again we have the author explicitly drawing attention to the technique being used in sonnet 14.

To link this chapter of the novel

> To John's departure, sketched before,
> Requires a flashback. (I should grovel
> At this cheap stratagem, and, more,
> My bard card should be burned.) Dear Reader
> In mitigation, let me plead a
> Drainage of brain. Perhaps you'll wait
> Till it's recharged? . . . You indicate
> I must continue with the story? . . .
> (A safe bet: if you've read till here,
> You must possess an iron ear.)

These references to the nature of the text itself and the dwelling on its 'textuality' in such a way that the narrator and the author appear to merge into a single figure represent a feature of post-modernist texts, as Thornborrow and Wareing (178) observe.

Another linguistic device the narrator employs to define the type of relationship with the reader is the use of questions to signal shifts in narratorial/authorial function from telling the story to probing the minds of characters, describing their background, commenting on their actions and relationships or even reflecting on human nature and life and death. Some of the noteworthy examples are

> Need John's life be so bug-infested?
> He wasn't always so alone. (2.13)
> His work's use does not disconcert him;
> At least, not much. . . .
> He'd clung to "standards," good or bad.

The narrator provides an answer to the question asked by giving an account of the circumstances that have made John what he is.

The second example is about the relationship between Phil and Ed.

> What does Phil see in Ed? Why does he
> Seem so committed to him? True,
> Once at a party, drunk and fuzzy
> —John should be shaken if he knew—
> Phil made it with a guy at college. (4.47)

But still: Phil's always been attracted
By vulnerable people; Ed,
Eager, confused, intent, abstracted,
Is passionate in both speech and bed. (4.48)

The narrator's answer in the two sonnets gives the reader an insight into the characters of the two men.

It is interesting to see that a little later the narrator asks and answers another question about the same relationship, this time from Ed's perspective.

Why is it then that Ed, unshielded
From passion's fallout (or attacked
By Cupid's minutemen), has yielded
His heart to Phil? The very fact
That Phil was married, and is living
With his young son, succeeds in giving
Him the attraction, in Ed's eyes,
Of someone sound and worldly-wise. (5.11)

One of the characteristic features of the narrative style in *The Golden Gate* relates to the manner in which the animals that appear are presented almost as characters in the story. This is most noticeable with the cat, Charlemagne and the narrator gives the reader Charlemagne's perspective of the relationship between John and Liz by means of a series of questions in 6.18 and 19.

How does John dare, the loathed intruder,
To breach the bounds of his domain,
Usurp his realm, or, to be cruder,
To rape his solitary reign
Inviolate since when, as a kitten
—Lost, ear-tom orphan—he had smitten
Liz's soft schoolgirl heart with love?
How dare John think—Great Cats above!
Cohabitation spells immunity?
That sordid catnip could replace
His mistress's nightly embrace?
And how, with cavalier impunity
Dare *he* share Liz's bed and, more,

Lock Charlemagne outside the door?
Is it then come full circle for you,
Old Cat, old friend, who pawed the door
Of a strange house till Lizzie saw you,
So many swift-spent years before?
Is it surprising that the kitten,
Famished and fearful, should have bitten
Her arm with hunger and relief,
Or proved half watchman and half thief?

Again in 6.21 we have the narrator trying to interpret what Charlemagne's purr could have meant by means of questions.

What did that purr reflect? The tender
Fealty of a one-person cat?
Or memories of nights of splendour
When with a snarling caveat
The territorial marauder
Scattered his rivals in disorder
To quench some she-eats arching wiles
Upon the clattering star-lit tiles?
Or, as he aged, the sweet security
Of love that mellows in old casks
Whose ebbing essence moulds and masks
The vintage of its youthful purity?)

Sometimes the narrator uses a question to signal a shift in narratorial perspective as in 2.29.

How could John know that Liz Dorati
(Ex-Stanford Law School, last year's batch)
Is neither cool nor stern nor hearty,
And much sought after as a match
By more than one well-heeled attorney
At the staid law firm Cobb & Kearny?

Here the perspective changes from John's to Liz's and helps the narrator to give the reader Liz's background.

Questions are also used to signal another kind of narratorial shift, namely the shift from telling the story to reflecting on human nature and on life and death. Thus following an account of how Chuck was affected by his parents' death in the accident, we have in 13.10

> Are the dead, too, defiled by sorrow,
> Remorse, or anguish? We who live
> Clutch at our porous myths to borrow
> Belief to ease us, to forgive
> Those who by dying have bereft us
> Of themselves, of ourselves, and left us
> Prey to this spirit-baffling pain.

Similarly when the papers and critics revise their judgment of Jan's work after her death, we hear the narrator wondering about how she might have responded to this kind of fickleness.

> Would it have given Jan some pleasure,
> This fat albeit fickle praise?
> Would she have looked at it at leisure,
> Stood at the mirror, tried a phrase . . . .
> Or would such flatulent bombast
> From such a source have made her scornful
> Of her own work? Or turned her head?
> Or left her cold? Since Jan is dead
> Survived by nothing but two mournful
> Cats, and her parents, and the stray
> Thoughts of a few friends—who can say? (13.30)

The birth of Phil and Liz's baby has the narrator wondering again about human nature. Why all this madness about babies?

> And how come even Mrs. Weiss,
> Who spurned Liz as if she had rabies,
> Agrees abruptly to be nice;
> What's more, consents to come and visit!
> Is it their helplessness? What is it? . . .
> Why are these egotists bombarded
> With kisses, hugs, and smiles to spare?
> Others, I think, deserve a share. (13.46)

Needless to say that the answers the narrator gives to the questions he asks clearly indicate a specific attitude to events and characters and their behaviours and relationships.

In addition to employing the devices of directly addressing the reader and using questions to signal shifts in narratorial function, the narrator/author also gives the reader explicit signals to help in understanding the narrative and textual structure wherever he thinks necessary. For example, when John's note to *Anne T. Friese* is returned with *Box Number Changed,* the narrator tells the reader that it was Jan who replied the ad in the name of Anne, which John finds out only after Jan's death at the end.

> Thus Janet (alias Anne)'s arranged
> Her creature's discontinuation.
> She feels the note she wrote for fun
> Would have been better unbegun. (2.24)

In 3.14 Paul crying for his mother leads to Phil thinking about Claire and their marriage.

> Phil puts his arms around him, kisses
> His grimy face and says, "Don't cry . . ."
> "Poor boy," he thinks, 'I guess he misses
> His mother even more than I.
> It's been a year, Claire, since your leaving.

Phil's thoughts take up four more sonnets. The narrator begins 3.19 with

> Such thoughts melt through the frozen river
> Of his sad mind, and yet out loud,
> Seeing Paul quietly weep and shiver,
> He says . . .

Thus the narrator helps the reader with an explicit signal to mark a shift from "the internal to the external view." (Fowler: 1977: 89)

A little later, the narrator/author feels it necessary to give the other side of the story of the marriage and introduces it explicitly with

> To adjust a portrait too one-sided,
> I ought to state that *in reClaire*

Informed opinion is divided. 3.25

Two more sonnets 26 and 27 are devoted to this purpose.

Yet another instance of the narrator/author directly telling the reader that the narration is moving backwards in time occurs in 6.2.

This story's time lens is retreating
Not with intention to confuse
But rather to update the news:
It is two months since their first meeting.
Liz has invited John tonight
To dine with her by candlelight.

Towards the end of 6.10 there is again an explicit signal that the story is returning to the point from where it moved backwards.

But since we're catching
Up with events described above,
We'll shun redundancy and move (6.10)

Directly to the morning after. (6.1)

In 6.14 we have the narrator directly addressing a character, John, with a warning, which indirectly but no less definitely suggests to the reader how the story is to develop.

Ah, John, don't take it all for granted.
Perhaps you think Liz loves you best.
The snooker table has been slanted.
A cuckoo's bomb lies in the nest.
Be warned. Be warned. . . .
So too it happens, now and then,
That a furred beast with feral features. . . .
Of that familiar brood of creatures
The world denominates a cat,
Enters the game, and knocks it flat.

Thus we find that devices like direct addresses to the reader, questions and explicit structural signals function as discoursal signposts that not only facilitate smooth reading and easy comprehension of the text but also convey specific attitudes to the events and characters in the story.

Just as the narratorial/authorial voice in a narrative text decides the degree of proximity between the reader and the narrator/author, there are specific features of narrative style that decide the degree of proximity between the reader and the fictional world created by the narrator/author. Seth uses three significant stylistic features to bring the fictional world created (characters, events and settings) very close to the reader and to enable her to perceive it with dramatic/cinematic immediacy.

The normal convention in storytelling is to use past tense. In contrast the use of present tense in fictional narratives is a marked stylistic feature since it is a special use of what is called "the historic present", which "describes the past as if it is happening now" and "conveys something of the dramatic immediacy of an eye-witness account" (Quirk et al: 1985:183). Seth uses the present tense for narration, description and comment in *The Golden Gate.*

As far as the story is concerned, it is only when the narration goes back to a time prior to the current point in the text that past tense is used. Otherwise the entire story is told in present tense helping the reader to witness the events from the position of a front row spectator. Thus we have

> He goes home, seeking consolation
> Among old Beatles and Pink Floyd. (1.8)

> He phones Phil, the first time in ages,
> But there's no answer. (Friday night.) (1.11)

> John kisses Janet swiftly, lightly. . . .
> They smile and part
> In friendship, with a lightened heart. (1.41)

> Two mornings after Janet fires
> Her postal charge, she's roused from sleep. (2.6)

> The pair are now rapt in discussion.
> Jan comes in, sees them, cannot hear
> What they are saying. (2.39)

The night is cold. It's late November.
They stand close, shivering side by side. (2.50)

A tow-haired boy sits with his father
Upon a rock that caps a hill. (3.2)

As Liz hears them play
Tears come into her eyes. (3.30)

Phil drowns vermouth and bourbon, sinking
Out of a world of loss and pain. (4.14)

Phil looks at Ed: intense, athletic,
Silent. (4.24)

Ed leaves on the kitchen table,
A note. (4.37)

The two shake hands and turn away. (4.54)
Paul now sees them, utters
A war whoop and insists that Ed
Playchess. (5.40)

And so
Ed stays on and, as day is dawning . . .
Packs bag and beast, and drives away. (5.44)

John reads the *San Francisco Chronicle,*
Sipping his dark Colombian brew. (6.12)

That night Liz works late. John retires.
She scans tracts on insurance law,
On Acts of God and covered fires.
With twitching hands and quivering jaw
John naked, bursts into the study. (6.23)

Next day is Sunday. In the morning
Phil drops in to see John and Liz. (6.38)

The monitors maintain a cordon
Across the road. All traffic stops. (7.39)

Liz stops, and puts the mike down. Twenty
Seconds pass. No one speaks at all. (7.48)

Ed, with a right hook swift and vicious,

Knocks Phil down. Dazed, Phil makes a slow
Lunge for Ed, who, with adventitious
Timing, swerves straight into the blow. (8.23)

They stare with loathing at each other.
Who just two minutes past were friends. . . .
They walk in silence. John's head reels. (9.16)

Phil lifts a hand to shield his sight,
And Liz with quietened emotion
Asks him how Paul is, and they talk
With their old ease, along their walk. (9.40)

and Liz, her earlobes burning,
Suddenly rises, and without
Comment or protest, walks straight out. (10.29)

He starts his car. When Ed cries, "Wait!"
John glares through him with transferred hate. (10.40)

He does. With startled recognition
He sees her face across the crowd. (11.39)

Jan sees a smooth, wave-worn sand dollar. (11.52)

John hires a small boat; together
They guide it out to watch the whales (12.13)

He squeezes through the reveling fever
Toward the phone, lifts the receiver. (12.36)

When the story moves backwards in time, we find the use of past tense, as in

Her family frowned at Phil's crude air,
Then shrugged, and tried to absorb their burly,
Rogue son-in-law who, curt and surly,
Splattered (to Claire's grief) needless yolk
Upon her nest of gentlefolk. (3.25)

Her mother's illness, the traumatic
Parley with John, Phil's long brief read,
Left Liz so drained, pale, and erratic
In thought, mood, look, and word that Ed
(Himself perplexed by John's behaviour)

Stepped in as psychiatric savior,
And steeped her with brandy for her good,
And soothed her as a brother should. (11.15)

The night John heard that Jan was dying,
Trembling, and dazed with grief, he drove
To the hospital where she was lying,
Sunk in a coma. (13.11)

Seth uses present tense to describe his characters and to comment on their actions and behaviour too. Examples are:

John's looks are good. His dress is formal.
His voice is low. His mind is sound.
His appetite for work's abnormal. (1.3)

On the tennis court
Or with his advertising rabble
Ed spouts forth a distracting babble
Of witty entertaining trash
Till his companions long to smash
Their rackets on his simmering cranium
Or seal his lips with editing tape. (4.22)

John looks around him with enjoyment.
What a man needs, he thinks, is health;
Well-paid, congenial employment;
A house, a modicum of wealth;
Some sunlight; coffee and the papers. (6.13)

When one considers how pain mangles
John, who believes he's duped by love,
When one considers that triangles
Such as the one described above
Lent five-star material
To Shakespeare and the Greeks, ethereal
Dream bubbles such as Janet blows
Of universal love expose
An aspiration somewhat artless
In one whose art's far from naive.
It's true that Jan does not believe
John's stance is reasonless or heartless;

She sees it, though, as rigid. Well,
Perhaps that's so; it's hard to tell. (12.3)

In descriptions of scenic background too, we find the use of present tense. Examples are

Two brittle oaks in dark rigidity,
Bare-branched and canted, crown the crest.
Above the rock with swift fluidity
A scrub jay flashes to its nest
—A cyan flicker where the greenery
Of mistletoe revives the scenery
Entangled in the generous boughs
Of its old host; and cattle browse
Along the moister gullies, scattering
As joggers . . .
It's dark. He drives. The street lamps glimmer
Through cooling air. The golden globes
By City Hall glow, and the glimmer. . . .
Of lights shines out across the water,
Across the bay, unruffled daughter
Of the Pacific; on the crests
Of hill and bridge red light congests
The sky with rubies. (5.7)

From the tall overlook, the indented
Shoreline extends in cliffs and bays
And promontories through the scented
Wind-sheared sage northwest to Point Reyes. (11.46)

In addition to producing an effect of dramatic/cinematic immediacy, the use of present tense for narration, description and comment (along with the conversational style) evokes the flavour of an oral narrative where the storyteller performs the dual functions of a narrator and a chorus.

The significance of the way in which speech and thought are presented in narratives has been widely discussed by literary critics and stylisticians. The use of direct speech, indirect speech and free indirect speech and of direct thought, indirect thought and free indirect thought by various novelists has been examined in detail by Leech and Short (1981) and many others.

What we find in *The Golden Gate* is almost always direct speech and very often without reporting verbs or even references to the speakers. Long stretches of conversation where only the actual words spoken are presented are quite frequent. Some typical examples are:

"You'll blow it badly
Till you clean up your Pigspeak act."
"Oh, come now, don't overreact,
Janet, you know I didn't mean it."
"Nor, I suppose, did the crude crass
Hall manager who pinched my ass
Last night. 'Cute chick. 'You should have seen it.
I punched his snout. 'To hook a chick'
Such porcine lingo makes me "sick."
"A venial linguistic tumor."
"It's not benign." "But it was just
A joke, Jan. Where's your sense of humour?"
"It's dormant since last night."
"Why must
You blame me for his roving trotter?"
"Because, sweet ostrich, it was not a
Harmless joke. Enough said, John.
You've got my drift. I won't go on."
"I donned machismo just to rile you."
'Well, you succeeded." "Sorry, Jan
Friends?" "Friends—of course, you fool, how can
You doubt it? Though I think I'll file you
Under 'Male Repentant Pig.'" (1.27)

"Hey, Phil, who's R?"
"Rowena." "Oh." "Tough player—fights on
Even when obviously too far
Behind to stand a chance of winning.
And even though at the beginning
I'd cream her, since she's had a go
At Russian, monsters like *zemstvo*
Have scored her a few touchdowns." "Do you
See much of her?" "Oh, now and then.

She has a thing for single men
As you know, Ed." "I never knew you
Thought of yourself as single." "Well,
Single, divorced—it's hard to tell . . . (8.18)

I sometimes feel they're both as lonely.
Oh, well, I guess it's time for bed."
'Phil, if—I mean tonight I only
Want sleep." ''Now, what's the matter, Ed?
Don't you—" "I do, Phil, but—" "But, what?" "It's
Just that." "Rowena?" "No, it's not. It's
Too hard to look, I can't explain."
"Ed, don't play games with me again."
'I love you, Phil—but my desire
Goes beyond sex. (8.19)

Such presentations of direct speech ensure that the reader 'hears' what the characters say without any intervention of the narrator/author in the form of reporting verbs or references to the speakers. It is almost like the spectators in a theatre hearing the dialogue in a play.

If at all the narrator/author uses a reporting verb, it is mostly the neutral "says" or "asks" with a reference to the character involved. Sometimes we find verbs like "smiles", "laughs", "grins", "frowns", or "nods", which are visual and sometimes verbs like "smiles," "laughs," "grins," "frowns," or "nods," which are visual and sometimes verbs like "growls," "sighs," "whispers," "mumbles," "murmurs," "shouts," "gasps out," or "bursts out," which are audible, which are used to preface speech that is presented directly. The use of such verbs again serves to make speech presentation dramatic and immediate to the reader.

When we consider presentation of thought in *The Golden Gate,* we find a similar directness in the manner in which the reader is told what the various characters are thinking. There are two kinds of direct presentation of thought (1) brief ones that take up only a few lines, often one or two and (2) longer ones that take up most of a sonnet or more. The first is similar to an aside and the second to a soliloquy and therefore both add to the dramatic quality of the narrative. Both are presented directly within quotation marks. Examples of (1) are

> She slits the packet to examine
> The postmark on each envelope,
> Thinking, "I wonder if he'll cope
> As sanguinely with glut as famine." (2.4)

> "She's lovely," John thinks, almost staring. . . .
> 'Handsome, all right, and what he's wearing
> Suggests he's just returned from church. . . .
> Sound, solid, practical, and active,"
> Thinks Liz, "I find him quite attractive.
> Perhaps." (2.36)

> "Claire's not to blame," thinks Janet stoutly. (4.9)

> But back to Ed. . . . "Well, I know
> I'll never hear from again,"
> He thinks with unaccustomed pain. (5.6)

> Liz smiles at Ed; then, startled, showing
> Signs first of shock, then bafllement,
> Thinks, "Surely there's some accident. . .
> How can . . . and yet, what other meaning . . .? (6.49)

> He sighs, gets up, puts on a sweater,
> An easier pair of shoes. "I'd better
> Leave this apartment for a bit
> Or I'll" (9.6)

> "I'm
> A fool," she thinks. "Here 1 am, paying
> Two dollars for a measly beer.
> How do 1 know that he'll appear?" (11.38)

Examples of (2) are

> Phil meditates on his condition:
> "They say that our maternal genes
> Determine our predisposition
> To lose hair. . . . If that's true, that means. . . .
> Suppose
> . . . Instead of losing hair, it were

To coat our forehead like a fur
And then usurp, in swift migration,
Our eyes, cheeks, lips. . . I guess, all told,
It's good that we grow bald when old." (3.3)
Jan sits in the Cafe Trieste
And meditates upon the pieces
Of her fragmented life and art.
'"The thing is, never to lose heart.' (6.34)

Grandma's old dictum's too simplistic
Of course, but what's my A to Z?
'Go with the flow' that nihilistic
Inveterate philosophy?
What happens when the flow stops flowing?
Do I give in or keep on going?
My love life's damned. My art is stuck.
I drink too much. My music's muck.
I'd better stop this maudlin listing
Or it'll draw me to the brink
Of—well, I guess that Cuff and Link
Confirm my reason for existing.
Oh yes, and friends. Why don't I call
John for a spiritual overhaul?" (6.35)

Thus the narrator/author presents both the external view of the characters in terms of their speech and the internal view of what's going on in their minds directly and dramatically.[3]

A narrative by definition consists of a series of actions and events in a specific sequence. An important stylistic device in narration relates to the linguistic choices the narrator/author makes in presenting the actions of characters and the events that happen in their lives. These choices determine the perspective from which the fictional world in the story is presented and thus influence the manner in which the reader perceives the fictional world created.

Halliday's analysis of how linguistic structure can be used as a means of representing patterns of experience (1985: 101-57) is very useful in describing this stylistic feature of narratives. According to Halliday, the grammatical system of transitivity "specifies the different types of process that are recognized in the language, and the structures by which they are expressed." (101) In English he distinguishes between three types of processes, namely,

(i) Material processes or processes of doing (e.g. *Mary opened the door),*

(ii) Mental process or processes of sensing (e.g. *Mary liked the gift),* and

(iii) Relational processes or processes of being (e.g. *Mary is tall*).

Material processes are further divided into 'actions' or doings' (e.g. *Mary opened the door), which answer the question* What did Mary do? *And* 'events' or 'happenings' (e.g. *The door opened),* which answer the question *What happened?*

Mental processes are divided into 'perception' or 'seeing' (e.g. *Mary notices the cat),* 'affection' or 'feeling' (e.g. *Mary loves the cat)* and 'cognition' or 'thinking' (e.g. *Mary realizes the truth).*

Relational processes are divided into 'attribution' (e.g. *Mary is pretty)* and 'identification' (e.g. *Mary is a lawyer)*

In addition to these three principal processes, Halliday identifies three other, subsidiary processes, namely 'behavioral' (e.g. *Mary sighs),* 'verbal' (e.g. *Mary says)* and 'existential' (e.g. *There are two cats with Mary).*

It is often possible to choose between different types of process to present the same thing. For example, the opening of a door can be presented either as an action as in *Mary opened the door* (with a mention of the doer of the action) or as an event as in *The door opened* (without any mention of a doer).

The different linguistic realizations reflect different perspectives of the same experience. Similarly, we can say either *Mary has two cats* or *The two cats are Mary's* or *There are two cats with Mary.* The first two are relational processes, whereas the third is an existential process.

In addition to the type of process used, the participants in a process and the roles they play are also crucial in distinguishing different perspectives. In a material process as in *Mary opened the door, Mary* is called 'the actor' or 'the agent' and *the door,* 'the goal.' If the passive form *The door was opened by Mary* is used, *Mary* is still the actor and *the door,* the goal, though the grammatical subject is different. In *The door opened,* which is an event and not an action, *the door* is called 'the medium.'

In a mental process as in *Mary liked the gift, Mary* is called 'the senser' and *the gift,* 'the phenomenon.' Though it is possible to use a different structure as in *The gift pleased Mary,* where *the gift* is now the grammatical subject, the participant roles are the same, i.e., *Mary* is the senser and *the gift,* the phenomenon.

In a relational process as in *Mary is pretty, Mary* is called 'the carrier' and *pretty,* 'the attribute' and in *Mary is a lawyer, Mary* is called 'the identified' and *a lawyer,* the identifier.

An examination of the story narrated in *The Golden Gate* shows that the linguistic structures that Seth uses present a unique perspective of the actions and events that constitute the story.

A striking feature of the material processes found in the story is that most of them are either presented as events, which do not have an actor or have non-human, inanimate or abstract entities as actors which act upon human goals. Some typical examples given below reinforce the dramatic/cinematic style used in the narration as they present the kind of vivid images that spectators perceive in a theatre or on a TV screen.

> the ill-judged toss
> Of a red Frisbee almost brained him. (1.1)

> The food arrives as soon as ordered. . . .
> His chopsticks fasten on beef bordered
> With broccoli. Enticing scents
> Swim over the noise, the greasy table.
> Two bottles each of beer enable
> Small talk and large, in cyclic waves,
> To wash their shores. (1.22)

> The fitful pen moves on the paper.

It pauses to delete a phrase,
Doodles a face, attempts to caper
Across a dubious word, but stays
Poised in midair. (2.2)

Brown paper packets, marked discreetly,
Fonn the *Bay Guardian* arrive
Each week: within lie, nested neatly,
A clutch of envelopes. (2.4)

The freeway sweeps past humming pylons,
Past Canterbury Carpet Mart,
Warehouses, ads displaying nylons
On shapely legs that make John start. (2.11)

Belinda Beale's acceptance letter
Arrives (with photograph). (2.21)

The seventh letter gives him pause. (2.25)

John's watch beeps out the hour of seven. (2.54)

Zucchini from the kitchen garden,
Potatoes, turkey, kiwi fruit,
Jell-O that won't consent to harden,
And cups of chocolate constitute
The evening meal. (3.21)

The lights have dimmed.
Throats clear. Brahms' A Minor begins.
The brisk allegro. Then a yearning
Warm ductile length of lyric spins
Its lovely glimmering thread at leisure
Inveiglingly from measure to measure
With a continuous tenderness
So deep it smoothes out all distress,
All sorrow; ravishing, beguiling. . . .
And on and on till silence comes. (3.37)

Instructions come from Mrs. Craven
With quartermasterly aplomb,
The piercing vision of a raven,
The animation of a bomb. (5.42)

The salt's mixed as the water is heated.
An egg's released upon the brine.
It floats! . . .
Now into each packed reservoir
A sluice of cooling brine is pouring. . . .
The lid's screwed tightly; sighs are heaved;
The label's stuck: the task's achieved! (5.43)

The fridge hums, happy with its diet
Of ice cubes. Clocks click time away,
Contented with its circularity.
The crackling fissiparity
Of popcorn on the stove returns
Him to the present. (8.11)

While Ed's words, wary, composite,
Short, closed, pointworthy, bit by bit
Chew up the board in ruthless nibbles,
Sealing Phil's options one by one. (8.17)

Art's knife halts in its potato-peeling. (10.8)

next the quiet
Moments of drinking, then a riot
Of simultaneous speech, the loud.
Sound cycles pulse out from the crowd. (11.8)

a car horn toots.
The car halts; out step beast and bwana. (13.39)

Another interesting feature about the material processes is that sometimes Seth uses parts or organs of the body as grammatical subjects, which again has the effect of making the images sensuous. Examples are:

But hand and eye deployed in daytime
Yield, when night comes, to ear and hand. (1.12)

The critics' common nose
Sniffs magisterially at her shows. (1.13)
A chilled voice on the phone inquires. (2.6)

Halfway

Through the third act, her dexterous digits,
With small attempt at camouflage,
Engage in passionate petrissage
Along his thigh. . . .
The curtain drops. (2.21)

Paul's eyes expand. His small head's bubbling
At this grand glimpse of a new world. (5.17)

While round him voices rise and fall
In oral goulash, Occam's call
Leaches his vision of variety: (11.10)

Other examples of some of the material processes, which present important events in the story but have either no actors or non-human, inanimate or abstract entities as actors are:

Phil's scorn of "country-clubbing rabble,"
His jangling views, his uncouth jokes,
And (once, at Christmas with Claire's folks)
His use of "queynte" to win at Scrabble,
Resulted in a virtual ban
On Phil from the whole Cabot clan. (3.25)

Post-marriage incompatibility
Of taste and style and interest,
Now hammering on love's fragility,
Exposed its contract to the test.
Phil's vigour, once his great attraction,
Exhausted Claire now. (3.26)

It happens that, a few months later,
A concert of three string quartets
Draws Liz back to her alma mater. (3.28)

A month goes by. Ed's tennis playing
Resumes. His quips resume. . . .
but in the end
The common doubt of those born gifted
With his uncommon looks prevails
And his unfixed intention fails. (5.12)

No tribute lamb chops can seduce

Him from his hate. (6.15)

Next morning comes John's ultimatum,
Not frenzied so much as resigned. (6.26)

In the court
Where an injunction's being sought
Against John's threatened operation,
The judgment has come in. (6.29)

Charlemagne's sent to Psycho-Kitty
Three times a week, and time goes by.
September gilds the bustling city
Once more, and autumn's lullaby,
Weaving through chatter and commotion,
Sounds dreamily from bay to ocean.
The world, for all its grief and grame,
Goes onward very much the same.
The fog thins out; the rain increases. (6.34)

The sentence they were offered roused them
To staunch remonstrance. (8.5)

The clapboard church with the white steeple
On a gray, frozen day extrudes
A complement of cheerful people. (10.1 & 11.1)

Out of its hiding place
Behind the door, with swift propulsion,
A gray and orange mass streaks by,
Chased by a black puff with one eye. (10.35)

The catalysis
Of trauma or euphoria jerks
Us into acts where fine analysis
Could fling a Frisbee in the works
(How often, though, such rash transactions
Prove happier than our prudent actions).(11.23)

Her card, a single pleading line,
Arrives, ill timed at Valentine.
This seals her excommunication. (11.33)

The flame of rumour's struck tinder;

. . . the fourth-hand news
Hits Jan, whom it does not amuse. (11.36)

And yet, the pattern of their greetings,
The counted hours that they share,
Drive him from his embittered brooding
Against the cosmos. (12.1)

No wistfulness but, rather, laughter
Tinges their speech. (12.7)

But week by week, as springtime urges
Him to the caressing sun,
And the rain lessens, and March merges
With April, and the benison
Of days, their tread, and their profusion,
Distract his heart from its contusion,
His visits to the bars decrease. . . .
His new companionship with Jan,
Confined to daylight, helps him span
The darkness safer from the danger
Of the crude misery that drove
Him to unknown arms for love. (12.8)

One Tuesday night, the cancellation
Of a performance frees the sheep
To savor the unique sedation
Of soundlessness and early sleep. (12.9)

The party, planned to start at seven,
Once meant to mark the show's success,
Will act now as a wake to leaven
Its burial. (12.24)

The mental processes in *The Golden Gate* form a major chunk of the story in that they not only give an insight into the characters' feelings but also often result in actions that change the course of the story. It is a significant feature of Seth's narrative style that these mental processes are also frequently presented using structures that have either inanimate or abstract entities as subjects. Typical examples are:

But "Girl" elicits mere frustration,
While "Money" leaves him more annoyed. (1.8)

Rather
Yellowed and frayed in recent years,
This scroll still brings Jan close to tears. (1.17)

An abrupt torque of pain and sorrow
Wrenches Phil's heart. (3.13)

But a melodious iridescence
Of joy today envelops Sue
In her Mozartian debut. (3.30)

But Ed's ascetic
Tension betrays his own unease;
And by now Phil's free-floating status
(Buoyed by spirituous afflatus)
Projects goodwill on all mankind (4.24)

Incomprehensible elation
Floods through their spirits, as the light
Dies with the sound, and it is night. (5.38)

Confession helps to ease the pricking
Of his restless conscience. (5.41)

Across Jan's face a veil of pain
Passes, but soon she laughs again, (6.36)

A troubled mask
Slips over Phil's face. (6.39)

The weeks have warped the placid gradient
On which is even wheels were set.
Neither the sense, at every meeting,
Of his heart's full and rapid beating,
Nor the abrupt and scalding rush
Of redness to his face, . . .
But something infinite and slow
And tide-like holds his life in tow.
The salt of human love upon him,
To it his leached will yields control,
Whether it stings or heals his soul. (8.7)

And it seems as if a curtain
Of doubt has dropped across his eyes. (8.8)

A sudden impulse to embrace him
Arrests his heart, but can't displace
What now amounts to an obsession
To clear the agenda at this session. (8.31)

John's volatile exasperation
His semi-rational unease
Finds self-fulfilling confirmation
Wherever his mind turns. . . .
Phil's salvos at High Nuclear Tech
And Liz's legal volunteering
Oppress John dimly, mind and heart. (10.15)

And then a frigid distance,
A disbelieving hatred sinks
Into his gaze as the handwriting
Nudges his memory, igniting
Cold glints of fury in his brain. (10.36)

but a tightness
Within his chest acts to compress
His breath, and to subvert all action:
The crowded room the old attraction
Phil drunk—inspirited—merge to move
Ed's heart toward his former love. (11.7)

The invitation
Liz sent him burnt his heart to frost. (11.24)

His hatred wilts his decency:
His mouth is dry: his lacerated
Welt-ridden ego's aggravated.
His will to bring grief on the heads
Of the incipient newlyweds. (11.26)

Selective sensitivity
To his ills, blindness to their feelings
Of equal injury, his dealings
With Phil and Liz to him seem just
Reprisal for their breach of trust.

Lonely, and injured in his pride,
His sorrow festers though denied. (11.27)

None of his woes will lead to weeping.
. . . unless, with his will sleeping,
In dreams, at two at night, the ploys
Of recollection in a madness
Of uncontrol set free his sadness
Into his pillow; and his face
Grows taut next morning with disgrace
With salt upon his cheeks, as shaming
As a wet dream—the spoor of tears
Insinuatingly appears
To pock his swindled features, maiming
His poise. (11.28)

Each day's accretion
Of labour settles on his pain
Its nacreous coat of insulation.
And if this trick of desperation
Is also madness of a kind
More sleight of hand than peace of mind
At least it numbs him to the treachery
Of those he loved. . . . But love. . . . John sighs,
And the thought hardens his eyes
That any falsity or lechery
If the heart's cold and stamped with scorn
Can be indulged in, or be borne. (11.29)

But now no current countermanding
The icy flow of his closed pain
Touches his coast. (11.31)

In San Francisco's snowless winter
The gray weeks rinse themselves away.
. . . A painful splinter,
Drawn in more deeply day by day.
Not of remorse so much, or fretful
Resentment, as of a regretful
Sense that when old friends fall apart
Things are not well—afflicts her heart. (11.32)

No tenderness can gash or fetter
One who's seen through it all before. (11.33)

John's heart burns
With an old longing. (12.10)

Tonight a quilt of peace surrounds him. (12.11)

an unease
Has seeped into his mind: the onus
Of his work troubles him. (12.17)

Back in her studio, John's perplexity
Increases as the minutes pass.
But all his suavity
Fails to disguise his heart's concavity. (12.32)

With a dim, unsteady
Terror of fact, his deepening grief
Shook from belief to disbelief.
The unforgiving realization
Of his own love now pierced his heart
So savagely and wrenched apart
His spirit with such desperation. (13.12)

In those first days, a taut emotion
Of guilt and panic seized his heart.
The vehement delusive notion
That somehow he had played a part
In Janet's death, and was ineligible
To share her dying, grew intelligible
To his despair-demented brain. (13.13)

As if some random psychedelic
Drunkard or lunatic or child
Had left a daubed and reckless relic
On his mind's walls, with bright and wild
And unaccountable lucidity
So forcible in their vividity
That his perceptions seemed unhinged_
Old images of Jan impinged
On his dimmed life. (13.14)

Some days, it seemed, the analgetic
Monotony of work relieved
His heart. (13.16)

Sometimes his unassuaged obsession
To find some pattern in, some cure
For Jan's death, led to an expression
Of prayer less to reassure
His heart with hope or superstition
Than, with quotidian attrition,
To abrade its pointlessness and pain. (13.17)

waves of yearning
Drench his taut body to the bone,
And a sick turmoil of desire
Stirs through him with a craving fire
For her. (13.20)

Such dreams, evoking
The present vision of his death,
Random and steep, without cessation,
Half terror and half consolation,
Infect his nights; and through his days
The pressure of his longing plays
Tricks with his eyes. (13.22)

The knowledge that he never mentioned
His love for her, or heard her say
That she loved him his well-intentioned
Designed to keep all pain at bay,
To shield him from the agitation
Of passion with the insulation
Of casual conduct, light and bland
Hurts like a nail torn from his hand. (13.23)

The nouns that function as subjects are often emotions like *sorrow, exasperation, unease, tension, woes, remorse, resentment, grief, guilt, panic, yearning, longing* and *obsession* and very rarely, *pride, tenderness and peace. Pain* is repeatedly used in different contexts with different characters. What is affected is repeatedly *the heart* and sometimes *the mind* and *the soul.* The most interesting feature about these mental processes is the use of verbs like *wrench, pierce, seize, sting, burn, arrest, flood. compress, harden, gash, fitter, fister, surround, envelop* etc., which with their suggestion of physicality and violence effectively bring out the depth and intensity of the emotions to which the characters are prey.

The style that Seth uses to present both the material and the mental processes in the story reflects a unique perspective of the fictional world created. It is a world where events happen without any apparent human agency, as if human beings do not have total control over the happenings. Events and emotions are presented in such a way that they appear to hold human beings in their thrall.

The picture is, however, entirely different when we consider the animals portrayed in this world. The animals have the pride of place here and with a will of their own, behave quite royally and human beings can do nothing but pamper them. The examples below show how the structures used with animals are mostly material processes with the animal as the actor acting on specific goals.

Each day for breakfast Cuff and Link
Have fish to eat and cream to drink. (1.15)

Jan relishes the warmth and savor
The deeds of Cuff and Link confer,
The love they deign to yield to her. (1.16)

But, sadly, Arnold Schwarzenegger
I got just one looks really strange:
His legs keep getting bigger and bigger
But not his torso. "Should I change
His food?" Ed asks with some disquiet (4.26)
The wary beast observes Ed coldly
Stares at the green and mottled pear
He proffers. Noisily and boldly
He crawls toward him, unaware
Of the loose leash that Ed is holding.
Ed slips it round him, gently scolding:

"Now watch that dewlap—mind those spines."
But Schwarzenegger undermines
All of Ed's efforts at persuasion
By jerking, clawing—until he
Obtains his avocado. "We
Are now prepared for an invasion
Of our quiescent neighborhood.
You want a walk? (The head bobs) . . . Good!" (4.36)

On the back seat the iguana's cowering.
At Ed's approach he flails about
With his long tail in fierce frustration.
Ed leaps back with an imprecation.
Only when pacified with quiche
Does the green beast receive his leash.
Yet smarting still from the indignity
Of his incarceration, Schwarz
Lunges and jerks in fits and starts
Of uninhibited malignity
(Bobbing his head in truculent show)
At guests as they prepare to go. (4.26)

The grizzled cat, grim and disdainful
Of human weakness, lets his painful
Love of his mistress-heroine
(Who saved his life once) shrive her sin;
But as for John, the old tom tabby
Scratches his proffered hand of truce. (6.15)

That night Charlemagne tries to tear it
Down, but defeated, head half cocked
In caution and concentration,
Turns his mature consideration
To where John's briefcase, custom-made
In Polish pigskin, has been laid,
Open, at John's desk in the study
And, using more of skill than force,
Deals with the matter in due course:
A disembowelment unbloody
But satisfactorily complete:
Reprisal sudden, stern, and meet. (6.25)

There Charlemagne with calm urbanity
Points out the well-scratched peppertree.
Avuncular, the soul of sanity,
With not a quark of jealousy,
He takes them wandering through the garden
Digging for gopher burrows. (6.29)

The baby's born in late September: . . .
The three wise cats admire his crib.

Here Seth uses verbs like *deign to yield, observe, crawl, undermine, obtain, flail about, lunge, scratch, try to tear down, turn mature consideration to, deal with the matter, point out, take them wandering, admire* etc. The iguana is described as 'smarting still from the indignity/ Of his incarceration' and lunging and jerking with 'uninhibited malignity.' The cat, Charlemagne is described as 'grim and disdainful/Of human weakness' and 'the soul of sanity' and is attributed 'caution and concentration' 'mature consideration,' 'skill,' and 'calm urbanity.' All the three cats are termed 'wise.'

Another important facet of the fictional world in *The Golden Gate* relates to the urban and natural backdrop against which the events in the story take place. Descriptions of the urban and natural surroundings also contribute to the unique perspective of life that is presented.

The following examples illustrate the style used in these descriptions.

The freeway sweeps past humming pylons,
Past Canterbury Carpet Mart,
Warehouses, ads displaying nylons
On shapely legs that make John start.
A cigarette ad, sweet and suborning,
Subverts the Surgeon General's warning:
A craggy golfer, tanned, blue-eyed,
Insouciantly stands beside
A Porsche-caged blonde; coolly patrician,
He puffs a menthol-tipped King-size.
John tries to curb his vagrant eyes

And heed the poet's admonition:
"Beneath this slab John Brown is stowed.
He watched the ads and not the road."
But in five minutes other features
Divert him: "Honk for Jesus." "I
Swerve to run over little creatures."
"The President is a lesbian spy."
"Nuke the nukes." "Fan of David Bowie"
Or "Here today—and gone to Maui,"
"I . . . winos," "I.L.A."
Or "Have you hugged your whale today?"
"Bartenders do it with more spirit."
"Old beach boys do it with good vibes."
John sighs, looks up. An ad describes
The Roach Motel's compelling merit:
"Roaches check in—but they don't check out!"
John thinks, 'That's what my life's about." (2.12)

He walks back in: the menacing garter,
The flinging of the white bouquet,
The canapés, the reminiscing,
The crush, the chaos, and the kissing,
The twirling pairs, the tilting cake,
The thirties tunes "for old times' sake,"
The vast permuted introductions
With older couples who appear
To be at ease with no one here,
The contradictory instructions
Fed to the caterers and the band,
Lure Ed back to a brighter land. (11.9)

Seth often piles up a number of items in his descriptions, as he does here and the effect is to build a holistic picture with each item functioning cumulatively to produce a dominant impression of the idea to be conveyed without using a specific word or expression.

Implicit in such descriptions is the satirical attitude of the narrator/ author, which is explicitly revealed in the descriptions of the way the art critics write about Jan's sculptures before and after her death (12.19 & 20 and 13.28 & 29).

A typical example of natural backdrop is

It's spring! Meticulous and fragrant
Pear blossoms bloom and blanch the trees,
While pink and ravishing and flagrant
Quince bursts in shameless colonies
On woody bushes, and the slender
Yellow oxalis, brief and tender,
Brilliant as mustard, sheets the ground,
And blue jays croak, and all round
Iris and daffodii are sprouting
With such assurance that the shy
Grape hyacinth escapes the eye,
And spates of Easter lilies, flouting
Nomenclature, now effloresce
In white and lenten loveliness. (12.5)

What is noticeable is the use of adjectives like *meticulous, flagrant, shameless,* and *shy,* nouns like *assurance,* and verbs like *blanch, burst, and flout* with flowers and of structures where *Pear blossoms, Quince, blue jays, Iris and daffodil, Grape hyacinth* and *Easter lilies* function as actors in material processes and are grammatical subjects. The piling up of details again creates a unique picture of the profusion that is typical of spring.

Seth indicates what kind of fictional world the reader will encounter in *The Golden Gate* right at the beginning in 'Contents,' where the fourteen lines constitute a sonnet. A striking feature of the language here is again the predominant use of events or happenings, not actions with human actors and the lack of definiteness and specificity of reference. Thus we have happenings like

The world's discussed. . . .
A cache of billets-doux arrive. . . .
A house is warmed. . . .
Olives are plucked. . . .
Arrests occur. A speech is made.
Coffee is drunk, and Scrabble played.

A quarrel is initiated. . . .
An old affair is renovated. . . .
The months go by; the world goes on.

It is significant that quite a few of these are passive structures where an actor is only implied. There seems to be some ambiguity here because the question that may arise is whether it is the characters in the story or the narrator/author himself who could be the implied actor/s or agent/s.

If the implied agent is the narrator/author, the inference is that here we have an omniscient narrator who will by either overt or covert means determine how the reader will perceive the events narrated, the characters depicted and the world created.

If the characters in the story are the agents implied, the impression created is one of events that hold a sway over people's lives, about which they can't do anything.

The nouns are all indefinite in reference, e.g. *a cache, a house, a speech, a quarrel, arrests, friends, coffee,* etc. The suggestion is that the events narrated could happen anywhere to anybody at anytime (the tense is again simple present). The concluding line reinforces the effect by implying that nothing changes whatever might happen.

The above description of some of the important stylistic features in *The Golden Gate* shows that some of the devices Seth uses like "self-referentiality" or conscious dwelling on the structure of the text, telling the story in present tense, and dramatic/cinematic presentation of events by means of sensuous images (often in very short sentences) are generally found in modern narrative texts, whereas the use of questions and other explicit signals of narratorial shifts to build a close relationship with the reader, direct presentation of speech and thought, overt and covert comment and reflection on human behaviour, and descriptions of the physical surroundings that provide a backdrop to the story are all devices that have always been found in narrative fiction and are often considered quite conventional. Thus there seems to be a curious combination of the conventional and the unconventional in the narrative style used.

From a discoursal viewpoint too, *The Golden Gate* displays an unusual mingling of modes characteristic of different literary genres. Written in verse (as sonnets with a conventional rhyme scheme), it tells a story and depicts characters giving the reader both external and internal views like a novel. In the telling of the story however, it incorporates some discoursal features that resemble the aside and the soliloquy and some that are like descriptions of stage setting ('The Shu Jing. One.' 1.20, 'Daybreak.' 2.51, 'It's Monday. Seven.' 5.6, 'Evening; Phil's house.' 8.1 etc.), both of which are typical of drama. Further, there is something cinematic in the way events are presented (Apart from the linguistic structures chosen, we notice that Seth does use expressions like 'Cut to dessert,' 'move out of focus,' 'let's shift our lens' etc.). Over and above all these is the speaking voice of the narrator/author who builds a close relationship with the reader using techniques that characterize oral narratives.

Works Cited

Fowler, Roger (1977). *Linguistics and the Novel*, London: Methuen.

Halliday, M.A.K (1985). *An Introduction to Functional Grammar*, London: Edward Arnold.

Leech, Geoffrey N. & Short, Michael H. (1981). *Style in Fiction: A Linguistic Introduction to English Fictional Prose*, London: Longman.

Quirk, Randolph, Greenbaum, Sidney, Leech, Geoffrey & Svartvik, Jan (1985). *A Comprehensive Grammar of the English Language*, London: Longman.

Thornborrow, Joanna & Wareing, Shan (1988). *Patterns in Language: An Introduction to Language and Literary Style*, London: Routledge.

A Mozartian Debut:
A Note on Music in *The Golden Gate*

CHERIYAN ALEXANDER

In the third canto of Vikram Seth's charming verse novel *The Golden Gate,* there is a description of a debut performance of a Mozart composition rendered by Sue Dorati. Sue's playing elicits from the narrator a lyrical tribute to Mozart:

Sue draws dark and mellow
Lyrical magic from her cello
In Mozart's last concert in D.
O loveliness constrained and free!
Ah, Mozart prince of music makers [1]

A few lines later, in the next sonnet, the narrator refers to the joy that "envelops Sue in her Mozartian debut." It is possible to read this as a disguised self-referential trope, one of several in the novel. *The Golden Gate* is not just Seth's first novel but a rare virtuoso literary performance, second only to its great 19th century precursor, Pushkin's *Eugene Onegin.* In choosing to write his novel entirely in the form of interlinked sonnets, Seth embraces the constraints of a demanding literary form while letting his imagination roam free across as wide a spectrum of human experience as can be had in one of the world's great cities.

Form in music is not merely a frame within which to house theme and content, but the shaping force that makes them yield the aesthetic elements latent in them. In a certain sense, one can speak of form as being identical with theme. For music, the discipline of form is a *sine qua non.* Without the structuring given by form, music simply cannot be. In poetry, the choice of forms such as sonnet, ode, villanelle and the like can be said to be analogous to musical forms such as the sonata, the fugue or the symphony. Some forms, such as that of the sonnet, impose a high degree of structural discipline while others, like *Vers Libre,* are less demanding. In traditional canons of aesthetics, the artist who is able to create good art by engaging with the challenge posed by a highly demanding form always receives high acclaim.

Seth, by writing his debut novel in verse, and by employing, in particular, the intricately rhymed "Onegin Stanza" made famous by Pushkin, declares his passionate interest in subjecting his novelistic imagination to governance by literary form. In thus embracing a "classicist" position in an era that is not very friendly to such gestures, Seth appears to be going against the grain, running the risk of having his novel dismissed as nothing weightier than a literary curiosity. That it is still the focus of serious critical and academic interest—quite apart from its continued popularity, two decades after it was first published—is evidence of its great literary merit.

The central theme of *The Golden Gate* is that of human relationships in all their varying states and moods—sometimes strong, sometimes fragile; sometimes harmonious, sometimes dissonant; always vulnerable and oscillating between joy and pain. The fact that most of the characters are materially prosperous, upper middle class, white Californians only serves to underscore the fact that money and wealth do not shield anyone from the vagaries of life. The "still sad music of humanity", as Wordsworth so memorably put it, may be heard in every social microcosm. In Western classical music, the only great composer who engaged with the full range of life's potentialities and vicissitudes, and represented it all without succumbing to a tragic vision of life—or becoming unbearably sombre—was Seth's acknowledged idol, Wolfgang Amadeus Mozart.

One of the most insightful tributes to the music of Mozart was paid by the Swiss Protestant theologian, Karl Barth (1886-1968) in his famous "Letter to Mozart" in 1956, on the occasion of the bicentennial of the great composer's birth:

"What I owe you, frankly, is this: whenever I listen to your music I feel led to the threshold of a world which is good and well ordered, in sunshine and thunderstorm, by day and by night. Thus you have repeatedly given me, a human being of the twentieth century, courage (not haughtiness!), tempo (not exaggerated tempo!), purity (not boring purity!) and peace (not complacent peace!). If [the listener] really digests your musical dialectics he can be young and become old, he can work and relax, he can be gay and depressed; in short, he can live. You know now, far better than I, that much more is necessary for that purpose than the very best music. But there is music which helps men to this end (*ex post* and only incidentally!) and other music which cannot help toward it. Your music helps."[2]

It is possible to see Seth's *Golden Gate,* then, as analogous to a musical composition done in the style and spirit of Mozart. Mozart's music gazes unflinchingly at the whole range of life, from the ecstatic to the tragic, and yet is never overwhelmed by any of the extremes. This graceful and nuanced Mozartian balance is the model Seth appears to emulate in the novel. It is also possible to see in the structure of the text the influence of one of Mozart's most influential predecessors, Johann Sebastian Bach. Bach was renowned for perfecting the musical form or technique called the *fugue,* a form that makes repeated appearances in the work of Mozart. The fugue is a musical composition that features several distinct and contrasting "voices" or themes that enter serially and are eventually played together in a harmony that holds each in a "contrapuntal" relationship to the other, all interwoven into a rich musical tapestry. The manner in which the contrasting stories (or themes) of John Brown, Janet Hayakawa, Philip Weiss, and Liz Dorati are contrapuntally woven together in *The Golden Gate* makes it a literary incarnation of the fugue.

Another feature of a rich musical composition (such as, for example, a symphony) is the presence of *leitmotifs.* According to the Encarta Dictionary, a leitmotif is a "thematic passage of music: a musical theme that recurs in the course of a work to evoke a particular character or situation." T.S. Eliot, in his essay 'The Music of Poetry," (written in 1942) points out the centrality of such recurrent themes to poetry as much as to music: "The use of recurrent themes is as natural to poetry as to music. There are possibilities for verse which bear some analogy to the development of a theme by different groups of instruments: there are possibilities of transitions in a poem comparable to the different movements of a symphony or a quartet: there are possibilities of contrapuntal arrangement of subject-matter."[3]

When we examine *The Golden Gate* from the above perspective, we find it replete with such leitmotifs. One vivid motif, for example, is that of the city of San Francisco, caught in all its changing moods (5.7, 5.8, 9.28, 11.46, 13.1, and so on). We are also presented with the "Cats" theme:' the "vineyard" theme, and the "food" theme, among others.

Taken together, the fugal elements and the leitmotifs cohere into the novel's vast symphony of the ups and downs of middle class life in one of the world's most cosmopolitan cities in the declining decades of the twentieth century. Seth's debut offering in the realm of the novel does indeed manage to capture the tenor and spirit of one of Mozart's great and graceful compositions.

NOTES

1. Vikram Seth, *The Golden Gate* (Penguin India, 2006), p. 67.
2. Cited in the internet URL http://www.etss.edu/hts/hts3/info18.htm
3. T.S. Eliot, *Selected Prose* , ed. John Hayward (London: Penguin, 1953), p. 67.

A Sonata in C Major
Vikram Seth's *The Golden Gate*

S. RAMASWAMY

Though the novel in verse is as old as Kshemendra's (11th century) *Padyakadambari* and *Lavanyavati* in India, the novel itself is a comparatively novel form in English and the novel in verse is certainly a novelty. It must be asserted at the outset that there is nothing 'Indian' about *The Golden Gate* except the name of its author. However, that aspect is outside the scope of the present paper. Pushkin's *Eugene Onegin* is the novel in verse that has provided inspiration to Vikram Seth's *The Golden Gate*. To put it in Seth's own words:

> Reader, enough of this apology;
> But spare me if I think it best,
> Before I tether my monology,
> To take a stanza to suggest
> You spend some unfilled day of leisure
> By that original spring of pleasure:
> Sweet watered, fluent, clear, light, blithe
> (This homage merely pays a tithe
> Of what is joy and inspiration
> It gave me once and does not cease
> To give me)—Pushkin's masterpiece
> In Johnston's luminous translation:
> *Eugene Onegin*—like Champagne
> Its effervescence stirs my brain. (102)

The characters in *The Golden Gate*—John, Janet, Liz, Phil, Claire, Ed, Sue and even the cats, Charlemagne the Great which surpasses Cuff and Link, the lesser representatives of the feline fraternity and even the Iguana named after Mr. Universe, Arnold Schwarzenegger—are not primary enough in comparison to California itself—symbolized by the Golden Gate bridge—as the presence against which the whole human drama is unfolded. Thus it is a 'Californian novel' in the best sense of the term.

The fact that *The Golden Gate* is written in 593 sonnets has obviously made it a technical *tour de force* and it has received rave reviews mainly because of that and other reasons, too. Rowena Hill, in her paper on *The Golden Gate* modestly subtitled "A Quick Look" (*The Literary Criterion*, vol. XXI, no. 4, 1986) has taken a summary look at all aspects of this phenomenal novel in an epigrammatic manner. What the present writer intends to do in this paper is to try to pay attention to one aspect of this novel—its form in terms of the 'Sonata form,' keeping in mind that the real protagonist of the novel is California itself—'C Major' to take liberties with a technical expression in Western classical music. Again, to quote from the author himself:

How do I justify this stanza?
These feminine rhymes? My wrinkled muse?
This whole passé extravaganza?
How can I (careless of time) use
The dusty bread moulds of Onegin
In the brave bakery of Reagan?
The loaves will surely fail to rise
Or else go stale before my eyes.
The truth is, I can't justify it.
But as no shroud of critical terms
Can save my corpse from boring worms,
I may as well have fun and fly it.
If it works, good; and if not, well,
A theory won't postpone its knell. (101)

Why, asks a friend, attempt tetrameter?
Because it once was noble, yet
Capers before the proud pentameter
Tyrant of English. (102)

Thus it is pretty obvious that to discuss the form of this novel in terms of plot, characterization, dialogue, style, atmosphere and philosophy of life, the good old characteristics of the novel would be as meaningless as talking about it in terms of dealing with it in the context of the types of novel like the epistolary, domestic, dramatic, the picaresque, the psychological, the stream-of-consciousness etc. A unique novel in verse like *The Golden Gate* deserves an unconventional treatment and hence this inter-disciplinary approach to *The Golden Gate* in terms of the 'Sonata form' of western classical musical tradition.

The relevance of the use of musical terminology in literature needs no defence. From Milton's *L 'Allegro* to Eliot's *Four Quartets* with its five 'movements' in each Quartet is too well known for any elaboration. Novels like *Don Quixote* have been rendered into Opera, Huxley's novel *Point, Counterpoint* directly employs musical terminology in its very title and Herman Broch's *Death of Virgil* has been described as a "prose symphony in four Movements." Thus an attempt to look at the form of *The Golden Gate* in the 'Sonata form' seems not only relevant but inevitable.

II

Vikram Seth himself has many references to western classical music in *The Golden Gate.* There are four references each to Mozart (40, 67, 68, 149), Bach (62, 76, 82, 180), and Brahms (65, 69, 71, 210), three to Schonberg (67, 68, 70), and one to Vivaldi (73). These references are more than casual. There is not only an incidental discussion of some of these composers and opinions expressed about them but they are related to the moods of characters in the novel. For example:

And Sue in recent years had been
So captivated by the cello
That bows and rosin and Mozart
Not beaus and roses, filled her heart. (40)

When Phil meditates on his separation from his wife Claire, he thinks of his life with her in musical terms:

> Sometimes we would light a fire
> I at the keyboard and you'd sing—
> Like the old days in the Bach choir
> Where we first met. (62)

If Bach brought Phil and Claire together, it was Brahms who kept them together for as long as it lasted:

> Now Phil hums a tune
> In a voice low, unedged, and quiet
> Until he sees that sleep has come.
> A tune from Brahms Claire used to hum.

When Phil has to play both father and mother to his six-year-old son Paul, he thinks of humming a tune from Brahms which his wife who is now separated from him used to sing. Thus Brahms is the bridge of memories for Phil. Again, in the main story of John and Liz in Sue's playing in the String Quartet is the cohesive force:

> It happens that, a few months later,
> A concert of three string quartets
> Draws Liz back to her alma mater.
> She phones John, "I've got tickets: let's
> Go down to Stanford. Sue'll be playing.
> Ed won't be there, despite my saying
> That sibling solidarity
> Concerns him just as much as me.
> I hope Sue isn't disappointed. . . ."
> "The program?" "Mozart, Schonberg, Brahms." (67)
> "Schonberg's an ulcer-generator."
> "Oh, don't be stodgy, John." "OK,
> It's a date honey." Two days later
> They hear the Ionian Quartet play:
> Four students. Sue draws dark and mellow
> Lyrical magic from her cello
> In Mozart's last quartet in D.
> O loveliness, constrained and free!

Ah, Mozart, prince of music makers. (67)

The family of Liz and their inter-relationships are tied up with their musical preferences:

Rich, bright, enrapturing, enthralling
Tapestry! As Liz hears them play,
Tears come into her eyes, recalling
That half-forgotten childhood day
When, at the insistence of their mother
She and her sister and her brother
Were press-ganged into lessons. Ed
Soon dumped his violin, instead
Sustaining through his adolescence
(By turns) guitar, trombone and sax.
Liz's viola bow grew lax.
But a melodious iridescence
Of joy today envelops Sue
In her Mozartian debut. (68)

Apart from Seth's own preferences and judgments of western classical music, like "Schonberg is an ulcer-generator" (67) or "floating on a slow tide of Brahms" (71) or "Mozart, the prince of music makers," (67) what is immediately relevant for the present writer is the fact that the application of the "Sonata form" to an analysis of *The Golden Gate* is more than justified in the light of the context of the internal evidence provided so far. Now let us apply the 'Sonata form' to his novel and take a brief look at it.

III

The importance of the 'Sonata form' cannot be overstressed, either in the discussion of how composers treat it, or in the necessity of the listener grasping its principles in order to appreciate what a composer is trying to do in his Sonata form movements. In its simplest layout, a movement in Sonata form will fall into four sections:

(a) Exposition: a presentation of a theme.

(b) Development: a discussion.

(c) Recapitulation: a re-presentation sometimes modified thematically and dramatically in the light of what has taken place in the Development.

(d) Coda: an 'ending' or 'tail-piece' to tie loose ends and to round off the movement.[2]

'C Major' is a key that emphasizes deep feelings. Mozart, Vivaldi and Rossini have been named in this context and these three have been mentioned by Seth also. This working definition should suffice here for a discussion of the form of *The Golden Gate* and a little more detail will be brought in at appropriate stages.

First of all, the 'Introduction' establishes firmly the locale of the novel—California. The Golden Gate Bridge, the Golden Gate Park, and 'the Golden State' as California is called in the United States, the entire far-west Pacific panorama is really the protagonist of the novel, in the same way as Dublin is for James Joyce's *Ulysses:*

Hail Muse. Dear Reader, once upon
A time, say circa 1980
There lived a man. His name was John.
Successful in his field though only
Twenty-six, respected, lonely,
One evening as he walked across
Golden Gate Park, the ill-judged toss
Of a red frisbee almost brained him. (3)
John notes the late September showers
Have tinged the blond hills round the bay
With a new green. He notes the flowers
In their pre-winter bloom. The way
That, when he was a child, the mystery
Of San Francisco's restless history
Kindled in him an answering spark
It strikes him now as, through the park
Wrested from old dunes by the westward
Thrust of green belt to the slow
Pacific swell, his footsteps go. (5)

San Francisco is described, "The unfettered city/Resounds with hedonistic glee," the Berkley campus, the Silicon Valley are mentioned, the Chinese restaurant and the freeway define San Francisco.

> But loosed upon the frenzied freeway,
> He gives no quarter, grace or leeway
> To lesser cars within the law.
> Tight-lipped, he hears the Peugeot roar
> Past little Bugs and harmless Hondas
> At 90 mph. (28)

John sweeps past on the freeway and in the evening, when he drives back on Route 101, it is either a traffic jam or "Commuting/Bumper to Bumper horns are hooting." (29)

Let us now move on to the Exposition: "With the Introduction out of the way the Exposition may start in earnest. The basic plan of two contrasting themes may be modified in countless ways: one theme only may appear, perhaps in two guises, in which case the movement might be described as 'monothematic.' . . . Often it is difficult on first hearing to sort out how many themes there are and where they begin and end."[3] In the Exposition of *The Golden Gate*, Seth introduces the theme of loneliness. John, Janet, Phil, Ed are all 'lonely' and indeed throughout the novel loneliness seems to be crying out for a solo performance and each character enters into a duet (which once in the novel literally becomes a 'duel!') between Phil and Ed. Though the theme of loneliness is the dominant theme, there are many other themes, like love—homosexual as well. However, it can be argued that this is also an Exposition in contrast to the duets between John and Janet, between John and Liz, between Phil and Claire (which is recollected in agony), between Phil and Liz, and between Art and Sue. John is described as 'lonely' in the very first sonnet of the novel (3) and as

> A linkless node, no spouse or sibling
> No children, John wanders alone. (6)

Janet remarks: "It's sad to see you look so lonely." (21) Even John's advertisement is significant:

Young handsome Yuppie, 26
Straight, forward, sociable, but lonely,
Cannot believe that he is the only
Well-rounded and well-meaning square
Lusting for love. If you, out there,
Are friendly, female, under 30
Impulsive, fit and fun, let's meet. (25)

In San Francisco which Seth describes as "the loveliest city in the world" (104) there are also these lonely, lovely lads and lasses "lusting for love." Janet is lonely though she and many others in California are very busy with their professions to the extent of being 'workaholic,' to use one of Seth's own expressions in the novel. Phil is lonely because his wife Claire has left him and he seeks first the companionship of Ed in a homosexual relationship and later at the termination of this homosexual affair, he turns normal again and gets married to Liz. Indeed, all the time, it is all happening in California:

Subdued and silent, he surveys it—
The loveliest city in the world.
No veiling words suffice to praise it,
But if you saw it as, light-pearled,
Fog-fingered, pinnacled, I see it
Across the black tide, you'd agree it
Outlived the magic of your own.
Even tonight, as Ed, alone,
Makes out Marina, plaza, tower
Fort Point, Presidio—he feels
A benediction as it steals
Over his heart with its still power. (104)

John, who is introduced in the first sonnet as 'lonely' is 'lonely' at the end of the novel after the desertion by Liz and after the death of Janet Hayawaka. Along with this theme is the theme of love in contradistinction with the theme of loneliness. John's love for Liz, Phil's love for not only Claire and Liz but for Ed—this is what is developed in the 'Development' of this novel.

Development itself is defined in these terms: "In the Development these themes are discussed. It is up to the composer to decide whether both, or all, themes will appear for treatment, or whether he will extract from one of the themes as much mileage as possible."[4] What Vikram Seth does in the Development of *The Golden Gate* is to 'extract' from the theme of love "as much mileage as possible"—in four 'Movements'—which can be thought of as (1) John and Liz, (2) Phil and Claire, (3) Phil and Ed, and (4) Phil and Liz. At the end of the fourth Movement, there is a rift between John and Liz and Liz marries Phil. All this, again, is the 'Counterpoint.' The 'Point' is California—with C capital—C Major. The human story of love and loneliness is unfolded against the magnificent backdrop of the city of St. Francis—the city of the Golden Gate Bridge.

> September gilds the bursting city
> Once more, and autumn's lullaby,
> Weaving through chatter and commotion,
> Sounds dreamily from bay to ocean.
> The world, for all its grief and grame,
> Goes onward very much the same.
> The fog thins out, the rain increases
> With less than customary zest
> Jan sits in the Cafe Trieste
> And meditates upon the pieces
> Of her fragmented life and art. (40)

In the delineation of the theme of love, there are the eternal triangles but with a difference—three different *menage a trois* situations. John's love affair with Liz is an interrupted melody with a discordant note struck by the love of Liz for her cat—the celebrated 'magnificat' (166)—called Charlemagne. The 'third party' in the homosexual affair between Phil and Ed is the memory of the ex-wife of Phil, Claire, who never actually appears in the novel. The third situation is the usual, normal (!) triangle of two men and a woman. Liz decides to leave John and marry Phil who was not only divorced from Claire, his wife, but who had the aforementioned affair with Ed, her brother. This is the main 'plot' of *The Golden Gate.*

Now we move on to the fourth aspect of the 'Sonata form'—Recapitulation, which is defined as: "After the drama of the 'Development,' the themes heard in the exposition are played again, but their characters are often transformed in the light of what has happened to them in the 'Development."[5] In Seth's novel, the Recapitulation can be taken as the Eleventh and Twelfth Sections of the novel. Here we meet the 'characters transformed in the light of what has happened in the Development,' mainly the altered situation of John who is again 'alone,' embittered and cynical but is 'comforted' to some extent by (what has happened in the Introduction and Exposition part of the novel), Janet coming back into his life and continuing from where they had left off. However, it has a tragic ending as Janet is killed in an automobile accident. Meanwhile, there are efforts made by Liz and Phil to remain friends with John whom both of them have 'betrayed' according to John. Thus the Development of the symphony in the novel form is recapitulated. San Francisco once again has been a witness to the human drama:

> From the tall overlook, the indented
> Shoreline extends in cliffs and bays
> And promontories through the scented
> Wind-sheared sage northwest to Point Reyes.
> Northward, Mount Tamalpais lowers;
> Southward, through leather ferns, wild flowers
> —Tangling and twining througl the lush
> Confusion of coyote brush
> And winter weeds—the blue Pacific,
> Unwrinkled as a pond, defines
> With wharves and cypresses and pines
> Three edges of the hieroglyphic
> Of San Francisco, still and square
> And sun-bleached in the ocean air. (257)

The last aspect of the 'Sonata form' is the Coda: "the tail-piece which brings the Movement to an end."[6] In *The Golden Gate*, section thirteen may be taken as the Coda. Here, the idea, that life goes on, has to go on despite everything is emphasized. Janet is dead but John *has* to go on. Months pass, Phil and Liz have a son whom they name John, and Liz writes a letter to John which says:

> We have a son,
> We hope that you'll be his godfather.
> We've called him John. We would far rather
> Have you than any other friend.
> Please speak to us, John. In the end,
> We'll all be old or dead or dying.
> My mother died two weeks ago.
> We thought perhaps you might not know.
> Phil and I send our love. Liz. (306)

This is the last but one sonnet of the novel and the novel ends with John's remembrance of the dead Janet.

IV

To sum up, Vikram Seth's novel in verse, *The Golden Gate*, seems to have been cast in the musical form, especially because it is written in sonnets. The 'Sonnet' and 'Sonata' and the Italian artists like Rossini, Puccini (43, 51) and Vivaldi, who are mentioned by Seth, convinced the present writer that its form could not be discussed in the traditional framework of the conventional novel. In the novel, Phil 'hums a sonatina.' (114) The Western musical composers who are mentioned throughout the novel are not there as ornamental appendages but as an integral part of the total scheme of the form of the novel. Since California is not only the 'locale' of the novel but the very spirit behind the goings on in the narrative, it was inevitable that this 'Cantata' on California had to be discussed in the 'Sonata form.' California in the novel is the 'Point.' The human story is the 'Counterpoint.' The passages dealing with Charlemagne the cat and Arnold Schwarzenegger the iguana, along with the lesser cats like Cuff and Link form the 'Divertimento.' The accord between Art and Sue is the 'Intermezzo.' The homosexual affair between Phil and Ed, to the present writer, is the 'Discord.' The whole Symphony of *The Golden Gate* under the very able baton of the maestro Vikram Seth is a singular achievement in Commonwealth fiction. Let Mr. Seth himself have the last word on his achievement:

> A week ago, when I had finished
> Writing the chapter you've just read
> And with avidity undiminished
> Was charting out the course ahead,
> An editor—at a plush party
> (Well-wined, provisioned, speechy, hearty)
> Hosted by (long live!) Thomas Cook
> Where my Tibetan travel book
> Was honoured—Seized my arm: "Dear fellow,
> What's your next work?" "A novel . . ." "Great!
> We hope that you, dear Mr. Seth—"
> "In verse," I added. He turned yellow.
> "How marvellously quaint," he said,
> And subsequently cut me dead. (100)
>
> Professor, publisher and critic
> Each voiced his doubts. I felt misplaced.
> A writer is a mere arthritic
> Among these muscular Gods of Taste. (101)

Since the publication of Vikram Seth's *The Golden Gate*, not only the "muscular Gods of Taste," the professor, publisher and critic but the general reader too has been echoing the initial reaction of the editor just quoted, 'Great.' Since the language of this novel, its rhymes and rhythms were beyond the scope of this paper, no comment was made. However, it must be noticed that the word 'Seth' in the above quotation rhymes with 'Great.'

NOTES

1. Vikram Seth, *The Golden Gate* (Delhi, Bombay, Calcutta, Madras: Oxford University Press, 1986).
2. This is a general summary statement about the 'Sonata form' and it is based on the information in *Guinness Book of Music*, Robert and Celia Dearling with Brian Rust (Middlesex: 1981, Guinness Superlatives), and *The Oxford Dictionary of Music* (Michael Kennedy, O.U.P., 1985).
3. *The Guinness Book of Music*, p. 89.
4. *Ibid.*
5. *Ibid.*
6. *Ibid.*

Intertextuality in *The Golden Gate*

RITA JOSHI

A hallmark of the postmodern element in contemporary culture and art is a sense of the merging and simultaneity of various cultures. Cultural hybridity is highlighted. Vikram Seth's work, set in various cultures where he has lived and identified with, highlights this aspect of postmodernity. Further, the various references to other literary texts in *The Golden Gate* do not just enrich the world of that novel in an ordinary sense: Seth deliberately plays up the references to other texts to merge the worlds of other texts into the discourse of his work and to make them a part of its identity. As Linda Hutcheon tells us: "No text is without its inter-texts."[1]

The most obvious reference in the novel is to Pushkin's *Eugene Onegin*. The author states in the novel: "How can I (careless of time) use the dusty bread molds of Onegin/ in the brave bakery of Reagan?"[2] The sonnet form of Pushkin inspired Seth to write a novel in verse. However there is also a continuity between Pushkin's fictional world and that of Seth implied in the relevance of the sonnet form to render both worlds fictionally: love, infidelity, a quarrel between two men over a woman, suffering, loss, death, social interactions in parties, eating and drinking as social habits form the subject of both novels. Eugene Onegin and his fictional friends become the silent Other of Seth's novel—The Golden Gate Bridge is a testimony to the permanence of an artefact over life—similarly, literary works make permanent the fictional lives of their characters which influence generations of readers and help engage bygone cultures with the contemporary era. *Eugene Onegin* provides a perspective, like the Golden Gate, from which to view the world of Seth's novel.

A text whose influence on the Golden Gate is not as obvious as that of Pushkin is George Eliot's *The Mill on the Floss*. The last chapter of the second book of that novel is titled: "The Golden Gates are Passed." In this chapter, Mr. Tulliver loses his property (including the Mill) to the lawyer, Wakem, and has a stroke; his son, Tom, has to leave school and the future of the two children becomes grim: "They had gone forth together into their life of sorrow, and they would never more see the sunshine undimmed by remembered cares. They had entered the thorny wilderness and *the golden gates* of their childhood had forever closed behind them."[3]

The Mill in the above novel is a symbol of permanence counteracting the flow of the river—just as the Golden Gate rises above the sea but can only exist in relation to it—the irony of the interlocking relationship between art/architecture and life. The characters in Seth's *Golden Gate* have also crossed over from the innocence of childhood to the pains and turmoils of adulthood. Philip Wakem is a lawyer's son in *The Mill on the Floss*—lawyers occur in *The Golden Gate*, and a central character, named Philip (suggesting Seth had *Mill on the Floss* in mind while writing his novel) eventually marries a lawyer, Liz, who is originally the girl-friend of John; here a role reversal takes place—the Philip of *The Mill on the Floss* loses Maggie Tulliver to Stephen Guest. Death and loss are a major focus in *The Golden Gate* as they are in *The Mill on the Floss*—Maggie and Tom die as does Janet, the young artist in *The Golden Gate*.

The Bible is a third recurring reference in *The Golden Gate*. The Bible represents in the novel an older set of moral beliefs from which most of the fictional characters in the novel are alienated. When Liz and John make love we are told: "The loving pair has bit the apple/ of mortal knowledge." (Sonnet 2.55) Ed, rejecting Phil's homosexual advances, says: "The Bible says, if a man lie, with a man, he must surely die." (Sonnet: 4.5) Father

O'Hare delivers an anti-nuclear speech: "By Christ's own sacrifice and passion/We cannot flinch" (Sonnet: 7.21). The Bible, like the Golden Gate, represents a permanent cultural influence on Western civilisation, permeating the modern world, questioning it and relativising it for the reader.

Various authors are mentioned in passing in the novel—Dostoevsky, Mann, Bede. John takes Belinda Beale to see Williams' *Cat on a Hot Tin Roof*, and the troubled, steamy passions portrayed in that play lend an intensity to the experience of the Californian characters.

Shakespeare occurs in two major references—John takes Wasp Bluestocking to see *Macbeth*. Bluestocking discusses "appearance and reality themes" and offers the thesis that "the Third Murderer is in fact/The central figure of each act." (Sonnet: 2.19) *The Golden Gate* concerns itself with characters exploring versions of reality and discovering illusions and exploring other realities. Also—as in the second of the above quotes—minor characters become major characters and major characters are relegated to the background in *The Golden Gate*.

> In Sonnet 2.24, a letter comes from Anne T. Friese (Janet) : "the king's third daughter"—obviously a reference to King Lear's youngest daughter, Cordelia; the Shakespearean heroine typifies a womanhood not available in contemporary times to John (who remains sans a girlfriend at the end of the novel). Here, Shakespeare's world has ideal characters and John's world in California is ordinary by contrast. Shakespeare's discourse is, by implication, literary—Seth's world is deliberately more prosaic—postmodernism foregrounds a consumer culture.

In the same sonnet a great American classic is mentioned: "She's just a name brought by the mail,/ Gone with the Wind"—the turmoiled times of the American Civil War described in Margaret Mitchell's *Gone with the Wind*—the havoc and tribulations in the lives of the characters and their attempts to rehabilitate themselves—become identified with the modern experience of the characters of *The Golden Gate*.[4]

Among popular cultural references—the reference to the songs of the Beatles stands out (Sonnet: 1.8). The Beatles, popular in the 1960s are a kind of anachronism in the 1980s of the world of *The Golden Gate*; nevertheless, the titles of songs like "Girl," "Money," "Taste of Honey," "Ticket to Ride," highlight the aspirations of the current generation of yuppies in the novel. The music of the Beatles lends a cadence to the language of the novel: the sonnet coexists with pop music. With such references we can see how the relativising of cultural identity occurs in the novel, impacting the novel and setting up the cultural components (here pop music and the sonnet) in a new interaction.

In similar vein to the Beatles, characters from cartoons are mentioned. Cats are significant characters in Seth's novel—and Seth refers to the well-known cartoon cat, Garfield: "Garfield, that egregious cat./Grows daily larger and more fat." (Sonnet: 2.38) Phil and Liz discuss the relative merits of the cartoon characters, Tin Tin and Asterix: "Haddock, Gorgonzola, Wagg, Moon rockets, grog, Red Rackham's swag." (Sonnet 9.26) The world of cartoons is an alternate literary culture—but finds in Seth's novel, the same relevance as works of high literariness impacting the influence and significance of that culture.

Non-literary intertextual references in the novel include classical music (Pavrotti, Puccini, Rossini, Bach, Brahms, Mozart) and art (Van Gogh, El Greco, Holbein, Goya). The sonnet form of the novel gains by association with the references to classical music whereas the characters in the novel get associated with the treatment of their subjects by the artists mentioned. A contemporary art form, cinema, also figures in the novel in the mention of Kurosawa, Alfred Hitchcock, Buster Keaton and the film *Tootsie*. Elements of ritual and feudalism, mystery and revenge and passionate love associated with these films are evoked and merged implicitly with other thematic concerns in *The Golden Gate*.

The number of references to other texts in Seth's novel testifies to the fact that literary works are enriched by other literary works and in the postmodern era this factor is celebrated, not played down, by the writer. The intertextuality of *The Golden Gate* places the discourse of the novel in a broader framework, opposing and questioning its particular grounding in a specific socio-historic context.

NOTES

1. Linda Hutcheon, *A Poetics of Postmodernism: History, Theory, Fiction* (London: Routledge, 1988), p. viii.
2. Vikram Seth, *The Golden Gate* (London: Faber, 1986), sonnet 5.3. Subsequent references are to this edition and the sonnet number is included in the text.
3. George Eliot, *The Mill of the Floss*, ed. Nita Kumar (1860; rpt. Delhi: Worldview, 1999), p. 167.
4. Rita Joshi, "Vikram Seth: In Other Places: An Inner Voice," *India International Centre Quarterly* (Delhi: Spring 1991): 55-65, on pp. 58-59 states: "Seth's close acquaintance with Western art and music is evident in this book. He refers to Catholic and Protestant Christianities, to chapel music, to Mozart and Brahms, to Holbein, Goya, Titian and El Greco, Henry Moore and Kurosawa . . . Alfred Hitchcock, Buster Keaton, the Beatles and Dustin Hoffman's film, *Tootsie*."

Crisis of Identity, Alienation, Aloofness, Loneliness and Death in *The Golden Gate*

SWATI PRIYA

Today in every type of media we find a discussion on the topic of aloofness, loneliness and crisis to identity leading to alienation and finally to death. With the advent of new machinery, technique and technology man has cut himself off from the society. Men have become slaves chained to machines like T.V., Internet, Mobiles, I-pads, Tablets, I-phones etc. They have no time to spend with their friends or devote time to sports or indulge in recreational activities; instead they have confined themselves to chat rooms inside the four walls of concrete and mortar. In this respect Matthew Arnold has aptly remarked in his poem *The Scholar Gipsy*:

For what wears out the life of mortal men?
'Tis that from change to change their being rolls:
'Tis that repeated shocks, again, again,
Exhaust the energy of strongest souls,
And numb the elastic powers.[1]

The scholar gipsy, having renounced such a life, is

Free from the sick fatigue, the languid doubt,
Which much to have tried, in much been baffled, brings

and is therefore not subject to ageing and death. Arnold describes

Before this strange disease of modern life,
With its sick hurry, its divided aims,
Its heads o'ertax'd, its palsied hearts, was rife

Modern man, equipped with new knowledge and technique, is leading a smooth-sailing, easy and comfortable life, if difficulties or problems come in their way they are unable to cope with them. Even if all their desires are fulfilled, they are still unsatisfied mentally. They deprive themselves of the laid back enjoyment of small achievement with family and friends. They are morally, mentally and physically drained out leading to different psychological disorders and disease; sometimes they even put end to their lives.

Many creative people have discussed this topic in their work. I would like to concentrate on one such modern Indian writer in English Vikram Seth. He is an unconventional writer, a trained Economist and a writer by his interest; belonging to the new set of writers of the great Indian Diaspora. He is an artist at home with different culture in any part of the world, absorbing their influences and giving expression to his influence in his writing, without even a hint of his being foreign to the respective native culture he has written about.

Seth takes up this burning issue in his verse novel *The Golden Gate* (1986). Before Seth many writers have voiced their views in their literary compositions on the crisis of identity, alienation, aloofness, death etc. To quote one such writer Diana Trilling in *The Women in America* (1965): "Today if we are to believe our fiction, the individual is not only isolated from society, he is isolated from everyone he knows, even from his own love partners. The connection between people . . . breaks . . . and man lives alone in marriage, in friendship, in business and in non-business."[2] Further she states: "The striking currency of words like isolation and affectlessness in the present day psychological studies suggests a new prevalence of the symptoms these words describe."

Seth's novel speaks volumes on topic of our discussion through the love life of five couples—John Brown and Elizabeth Dorati, Philip Weiss and Claire, Philip Weiss and Edward Dorati (Ed), Philip Weiss and Elizabeth Dorati and John Brown and Janet Hayakawa.

The central figure of *The Golden Gate* is John Brown, with whom the novel begin and ends, he is an isolated and lonely person longing for a life partner to share life with after the death of his mother:

> Twenty-six, respected, lovely,
> One evening as he walked across
> Golden Gate Park. . .
> The thought, "If I died who'd be sad?
> Who'd weep? Who'd gloat? Who would be gold?
> Would anybody.[3]

John is blond-haired, good-looking, healthy, employed, ambitious, sound, solvent self, self-made, possessive and depressed person. He is a young man of twenty-six and is described as aloof, prim and lovely. He has graduated from Berkley in Computer Science and now is working as Computer Programmer Executive in the area of nuclear research at San Francisco in Silicon Valley. He craves for a healthy family life that will cushion his solitude:

> A link less node, no spouse or sibling,
> No children—John wanders alone
> Into an ice-cream parlor. (1.35)

His life has grown dull the day he left college. He is a typical representative of the middle-class family whose parents are busy in their job to maintain high standards of living at the expense of warmth and love to their child. He always craved for his mother's love but got none. John is ordinary young man well educated, conservative, economically well to-do American Yuppie who suddenly finds sinking deep into the ocean of despair and loneliness. When he is encouraged by an old college friend, Janet Hayakawa, his ex-lover, a painter and sculptor by profession and a drummer in a band called 'Liquid Sheep' as a hobby, John decides to put up an advertisement in the local newspaper after Janet's advice, which will be like the idea that came in his mind:

Don't bank too much on youth.
Your rookie season is drawing
to an end. . . .
Start to make a sense when at the brink of thirty dome,
We pause to scan.

Further, Janet adds that we pray to:

God for a life-partner after
Hope, trial and search
To grant us someone who will do.
For love, and who may love us too
While those who wait, as age advances,
Aloof for Ms. or Mr. Right
Weep to themselves in the still night. (1.36)

His ideas of advertisement are transformed into writing by Janet. And with consent of John, Janet takes out advertisement in *Bay Guardian*, Newspaper, which reads:

Young handsome yuppie,
Straight, forward, sociable, but lonely,
Cannot believe that he's the only
Well-rounded and well-meaning square
lusting for love.
If you, out there,
Are friendly, female, widower?
Impulsive, fit and fun, let's meet
Be rash. Box. . . . (2.20)

John after constant change of partners; almost like the game of musical chairs, undergoes few tantalizing amorous experiences, then he is confronted with two eccentric candidates for marriage, first is Wasp Bluestocking. Seth tells us that she is an intellectual bore because of the constant use of French jargon. On the next Saturday, he meets another girl, Belinda Beale who turns out to be a highly sex conscious, sex-obsessed almost sex-mad in her first encounter with John.

After having been disillusioned in his adventure with the two ladies, John finds a suitable companion in Elizabeth Dorati, twenty-seven year old Catholic Christian, the charming, intelligent, young, urban, lawyer who graduated from Stanford Law School, an Attorney in a Law Firm:

> I'm friendly, female,
> Well-rounded too, and somewhat square
> I've not yet known romantic heaven
> But habour hopes of getting there. (2.28)

She belongs to a down to earth Italian immigrant wine growing family:

> Liz spends her weekends at her folks:
> A nine yard where she reads and soaks
> The sunlight of Sonoma Country,
> Talks to her dad of must and vine
> Her heart, her knowledge, or her skin
> She bloomed unhardened by her beauty. (2.28)

Here, she lives with her parents—Mike Dorati and Maria Dorati and also with her two siblings—her brother Edward, her sister Sue and her cat Charlemagne. Her mother always dreams of her getting settled.

When these loveless people meet John Brown and Elizabeth Dorati meet, their relationship seems to the readers, to be proceeding on the best of terms, to the extent that they are investigating the possibility of buying a house for them to start a family-life:

> They go to the ballet together,
> See movies once or twice a week,
> . . . now we see
> Pouring over want ads,
> Searching the dossiers of
> Real estate agents. (7.9)

But their love life has to pass through certain test of life and destiny. Elizabeth's cat Charlemagne creates a rift in their relationship as John does not like the presence of the cat. Though Liz is dynamite in bed, John is unhappy because of her extravagant and excessive obsession for Charlemagne, the anti-nuclear cat. The cat too resents the presence of John, the intruder who dared to:

breach the bound of his domain
Usurp his real, or, to be cruder,
To rape his solitary reign. (7.9)

To get answers to all the break-up to follow in the novel, we have to do a keen analysis of love-life of another character in this novel who commands the same attention as the main protagonist John. He is none other than ex-room mate of Berkley and also a close college friend of John, Philip Weiss. He is twenty-eight years old atheist Jew. Philip has worked in the Lungless Labs—a place which breeds bombs as Nuclear Engineer in Datatronics and a computer expert. He gives up his job because it troubled his conscience to work in a bomb-making factory. He forms an anti-nuclear group and raises up the issues by taking up peaceful marches almost like Mahatma Gandhi's Non-Violence processions against the rule of Britishers in India. The demonstrators carry the placards which read:

'I am my brother's keeper,'
Nice folks don't use nukes,
Work for life, not death. (3.19)

Philip was married to Claire, a protestant Christian for six years and has a son named Paul. He invested in buying a piano, furniture, Ford Capri Insurance policies etc. His home was what they prayed to have. But after six years Claire divorced him on the pretext of his dominating nature and also because of his lustful eye on men (i.e. Philip's homosexual and heterosexual behaviour). Claire never visits her son Paul neither sends any gifts because it will create anxiety in the mind of the small boy but his craving for his mother's love and desire to find united love of his parents has created certain doubts, raised few questions and made him emotionally insecure when he asks his father Philip:

'No Paul, She's gone away.'
'Forever?'
'I just can't tell you, son-but never think you're alone.'

'You've got me.'
'When will you leave me?'
Phil, shocked stares. (9.15)

This question itself raises issues of family-life in modern nuclear family, degradation of family system and parenting in developed countries like America.

Due to friendship with John, Philip meets Elizabeth's family members in a family reunion for Thanksgiving. There Phil meets Ed, brother of Liz, Ed is twenty-three years old man with sissified appearance. This meeting gives birth to a third love-life between Philip and Edward. Ed gives Phil passionate company not only in conversation but also in bed. Their relationship is born out of need and infatuation. Elizabeth takes her brother Ed and Phil affair casually and thinks it improper to interfere in their personal matter. But John holds an anti-homosexual opinion thinking that gay life is irreconcilable to the family life. He is of the view that one is programmed to mate with opposite sex. He has the Christian orthodox belief in matter of love marriage and sex, so he is surprised and disgusted with Phil and exclaims:

Oh! Jesus! Phil, but you are married . . .
Oh! Jesus! Phil—what do you find
In—what do two men do together?

But Phil is not like John, he believes in heterosexuality; nor does he share Vittorio's view in Andrew Holleran's novel *Nights in Aruba*: "You can have boys that, or you can have the pleasure of family life. But you can't have both."[4]

Phil (Philip) does not agree with the view that Gay-life and family-life are mutually exclusive or that one is the enemy of the other. For him homosexuality and heterosexuality are not substitutes but complementary to each other. This becomes clear through Phil's discourses which are attempts not only to justify but even glorify homosexuality:

When your heart's
Aching with desire
Should something that

You've somewhere read
By someone two millennia dead
Convince you that your heart's a liar. (8.33)

Phil asks Ed not to play the game of love by other's rules. Finally Phil, an indefatigable commentator on this topic, voices his monistic or holistic approach to the object of his sex when he says:

Love whole or else
It's nothing I can't see you Ed,
As their disembodied soul. (8.34)

He breaks out of totemic world of his forefathers and *The Bible* and enters into the rational world of science where sexual expression is free from all religious taboos. He has never bothered about convention in his life. Seth has described at length their night spent together, their magnetic draw to each other, their physical encounters, their caresses and their love-making. Phil and Ed are attracted to each other erotically and at some points they even sound like man and woman or lover and beloved very much in love. Phil and Ed's affair runs parallel with John and Elizabeth's affair in the novel. Their love life too tastes the sour reality of break-up. One day Phil and Ed are lovers and the next day Phil is gagged by sacramental text and this leads to quarrel. Gradually this affair turns defunct. At the end of this homosexual relationship Phil says:

I loved a woman and was dropped
I loved a man—and that also flopped. (8.19 & 20)

One is surprised to find a fourth love story building up in the novel. One also wonders what reasons are leading to this affair. The answer is because of crisis in relationship and alienation a love affair develops between two casual acquaintances—Philip Weiss [Phil] and Elizabeth Dorati [Liz], after the end of Phil and Ed affair. Elizabeth comes closer to Phil to support him emotionally and get consoled in return, because John Brown her lover left her in a burst of jealousy due to her excessive love for her cat.

This affair aggravates John's feeling of loneliness and gives him a sense of injured pride; makes him more loveless and his life more painful and difficult than before he met Elizabeth. To overcome this crisis and to come out of his depression, John tries to re-kindle his relationship with his former beloved and college friend Janet Hayakawa, an artist of Japanese origin. Janet is saddened by the way John's friendship and his love life have all gone astray; but she is too busy in her artistic life, too hurried to shower more than sympathy for John. This is the last love-affair depicted by Vikram Seth in this novel.

Meanwhile, Elizabeth and Philip decide to get married, Phil who bluntly considers passion: "a prelude to disaster" (11.20) Later on, Philip declares to marry Elizabeth because every human being needs a companion, somebody to rely upon, to share their life and their emotion with. Elizabeth eschews on untrustworthy passion and finally marries her friend, Philip, saying:

> And I'd far rather
> Marry a man who's a good father. (2.24)

Meanwhile, John and Janet finally realize the love and bonding between them; so they deeply regret his and her failure to express their feelings, preferring "the isolation of casual conduct, light and bland." (11.22) They were about to settle down in their life when the final and fatal blow comes in the form of a car accident in which Janet dies and John is left all alone once again. Phil tells his wife Liz:

> The fact is, he is so isolated
> By all his pain and bitterness
> There's not much we can do,
> I guess. (13.43)

Philip and Elizabeth are shown jubilant over the addition of a new member to their family; 'his house-hold greets its newest member with vast jocosity and joy.' John slowly and painfully finds the strength to face and accept his past, drying his tears and clearing his throat to get a meaning to his life. He is invited to become Godfather to Liz and Phil's child. And this birth somehow compensates the awareness of his fragility faced with the death of so many people connected to him—Janet Hyakawa, Mrs. Dorati, Dr. Matt Laymont and his wife. The novel begins with John as a lonely, depressed and dispirited man walking across the golden gate and ends with him depleted by his pain on loss of his beloved. Emptiness leads to emptiness. There is nothing left with him except the imaginary voice of Janet who is no more:

> I'm with you John,
> You are not alone. (13.48)

Vikram Seth succeeds in maintaining a perfect balance between a sympathetic understanding of the human predicament: lack of communication between people involved in a relationship, the anguish of loneliness and isolation in the world of promising happiness and economic stability and least contentment of satisfaction and lack of self-realization these all slowly lead them to the narrow dark lane towards the world of alienation or total aloofness. People become alien to one another, even husband becomes alien to his wife, lover to his beloved, children to their parents and family and vice versa and slowly this spreads like a contagious and contaminated disease engulfs the whole world. Those involved in this depart, dessert and break-off the shackles of relationship because they think that they got involved in a relationship in haste or are bound by blood relationship. They are dissatisfied, mutually incompatible and ill-adjusted after staying together for some time or few years. They question their status in their relationship, question their identity, want their space and freedom to do what they want without any expectation of any kind, monetary or emotional. These feelings slowly and silently like a white termite eat away the warmth of emotion in the relationship and people drift apart like two parallel lines that never meet. This emotional and psychological turmoil makes people commit suicide or even make them insane. Alienation also causes the death of love, family and married life against the glittering backdrop of economic prosperity and glamour around.

NOTES

1. Matthew Arnold, *The Scholar Gipsy*, Arthur Quiller-Couch, ed. *The Oxford Book of English Verse: 1250-1900* (1919).
2. Diana Trilling, *The Woman in America* , Volume 3 of Daedalus library Beacon paperbacks, Editor Robert Jay Lifton (Houghton Mifflin, 1965), Original from the University of CaliforniaDigitized 4 Jan 2007.
3. Vikram Seth, *The Golden Gate* (Delhi: Penguin, 1986), 1.1
4. Andrew Holleran : *Nights in Aruba* (Bantam reprint, 1990), p. 107.

Alienation and Homecoming: A Search for Identity in Vikram Seth's *The Golden Gate* and *An Equal Music*

SAUMITRA CHAKRAVARTY

In the era of globalization, one is expected to have multiple identities that require him to be at ease everywhere and at home nowhere, because the concept of home itself implies rootedness. Whereas earlier writers in exile had to choose between homeland and the land of exile, better opportunities and recent trends of globalization have made writers like Vikram Seth, Amitav Ghosh, Meena Alexander, Sujata Bhatt and many others like them relatively unaware of what Salman Rushdie calls an exile's wistful tendency of building 'imaginary homelands,' 'Indias of the mind' since they have embraced several countries and cultures, including their own. Rushdie claims that physical separation from the motherland makes it impossible to reclaim or recreate the land that the exile has lost.[1] Seth, on the other hand, has lived in China, Britain, the United States and back home in India. In fact, the three sections of his *Humble Adminstrator's Garden* are represented by three trees, each symbolical of a different country, the wutong of China, the neem of India and the live-oak of America, highlighting its author as a global citizen. Similarly, *Beastly Tales from Here and There* contains poems based on fables—two each from India, China, Greece, Ukraine and the last from the imaginary land of Gup. As a result, for such writers as Seth and Ghosh, the process of acculturation is a continuous one, as they move across countries and continents, or return to their own.

Yet the search for identity is central to the works of Vikram

Seth, as central as it is to some of Amitav Ghosh's novels. Samuel Huntington, in *The Clash of Civilizations*, says, 'The 1990's have seen the eruption of a global identity crisis. Almost everywhere one looks, people have been asking, "Who are we?" "Where do we belong?" and "Who is not us?"'[2] He goes on to say that the search has widened to include that for roots and connections that is man's defence against the unknown. So today's global citizens for all their multiple identities have a lurking sense of uncertainty. Janet Hayakawa in Seth's *The Golden Gate* has a Japanese grandmother, with a 'pauper migrant's menial life' and a strong sense of humour and values which helps her build a fortress against the ache of exile.[3] Uncle Shanti in *Two Lives*, has traversed several continents, is wedded to a German Jew and has strong Indian bonds. Julia Hansen in *An Equal Music*, is part English, part Austrian, married to a rich American banker and seemingly at home in all three countries. And though they probably do not suffer from what Rushdie calls stereoscopic vision instead of whole sight about their own country or countries, on the whole the sense of alienation or loss cannot be denied. Like the image of the whales migrating in pods and pairs in *The Golden Gate*, the global citizen of today moves to and fro in search of better living and exposure. Such a writer today may thus find it increasingly difficult to define his identity, but he undoubtedly has within himself a sanctum sanctorum, he calls 'home.' He therefore inhabits what A.K. Ramanujan calls, two different worlds, 'the one within, the one without.'[4] How then, does one define one's cultural identity in environments as diverse as those demanded by such a situation? Two alternatives surface: either one may submerge oneself in the broader or adapted identity and return as escape or safe haven to the narrower one, or one may identify so totally with one's own closeted idea of self that one tends to isolate himself from the world around. The latter is a dangerous trend and may qualify for what Vikram Seth defines as the ostrich syndrome in his verse-novel, *The Golden Gate*. This essay is an attempt to unravel the tangled web of identity in two of Vikram Seth's works, *The Golden Gate* and *An Equal Music.*

Flitting to and fro between country and country, the global citizen of today may suffer from a fractured identity, unable to assimilate either into the host culture or into his diasporic community within the host culture. He cannot integrate with his motherland either, though he may be only a temporary resident abroad. This is in itself a loss quite different from that suffered by an expatriate sheltered within a diasporic community which may help to blunt what Seth calls the ache of exile. In *The Humble Administrator's Garden*, Seth's sense of loss as a result of being continuously on the move across countries and continents is expressed through an inner fear and anxiety, 'They have left me the quiet gift of feeling/ I am consumed by fear chilling and searing.'[5] In *Two Lives*, unable to focus on his Ph.D. at Stanford due to his many commitments, Seth confesses to wave upon wave of nostalgia for home and an inner sadness at having missed the company of his sister Aradhana in her formative years. In *The Golden Gate*, John realizes how lonely life can be at the top. Having achieved too much too soon, he is like Eugene Onegin in Pushkin's poem (the verse-narrative which is Seth's acknowledged source of inspiration), which speaks of 'spleen, the scourge of Britain/ or Russia's chondria.'[6] The malaise of good life in a big, busy city catches up with John and he is left with nothing but 'work and the syndrome of possessions.' (*GG* 2.13) At weekends, he is lonely and restless. In a restaurant or a movie, he is an outsider glimpsing, but never tasting human relationships. Like Onegin again, who

> read and read—no satisfaction:
> here's boredom, madness or pretence,
> here there's no conscience, here's no sense;
> they're all chained up in different fetters. (*EO* I lxiv)

John feels the big city impinging upon his consciousness, but has neither conscience nor sensitivity enough to break either those fetters or his own complacence. As a result he remains a perpetual refugee, unable to build a home or enrich his relationships.

Unable to suppress their instinctive craving for home and for roots, the major characters in these novels feel a sense of alienation overriding the success and achievement acquired away from home. The simultaneous existence in the two worlds, 'within' and 'without' is thus generally expressed in two stages in the two novels under consideration in this paper—the movement towards a metropolis in search of better opportunities which the suburban home cannot provide, and a consciousness of outsiderness or even fringe existence in that metropolis, due to an awareness of one's own limitations of background. These characters search for roots in exile, however temporary that might be. Alienated as outsiders, they also tend to define their identity in opposition to the 'other.' Seth tries to project these definitions through a series of binary symbols in his novels—homosexual/bisexual, Jewish/ Gentile, alienation from/ integration into the mainstream American identity in *The Golden Gate* and solo/ensemble, suburban/metropolitan, working class/ upper class in *An Equal Music*.

John's childhood friend, Philip Weiss in *The Golden Gate* or Michael Holme in *An Equal Music*, have risen from working class origins and made a foray into the metropolis in search of better opportunities. Michael is a butcher's son, who has made a successful career in chamber music, playing with a trio or a quartet in the world's culture capitals. Yet his humble origins tend to overtake and finally defeat him. For Philip Weiss, a Jew and a bi-sexual, his marriage collapses when Claire Cabot who had earlier loved him for his rough and burly appearance and his straightforward ways, capitulates to the objections of her genteel-Gentile Cabot clan. Like Jimmy Porter in Osborne's *Look Back in Anger*, holding his upper class wife Alison to ransom, Philip is guilty of having splattered 'needless yolk/ Upon her crowd of gentlefolk.' (*GG* 3.25) His bi-sexuality is his armour against heartbreak and upper class rejection just as his active association with the Peaceniks, after giving up a lucrative job in

Datatronics, is his protest against mainstream American policy of imperialism, nuclear arms race and war-mongering. Michael Holme feels his working class identity closing in upon him with every encounter with authority. Whether it be the world-famous musician Carl Kall his mentor-turned-dictator, Julia's Oxford-don father, an air hostess who downgrades him or a police-woman asking him to keep off the grass, any show of authority instinctively raises his hackles. Michael enters polite, upper-class society—the world of playing bridge, learning foreign languages, visiting art galleries and museums—with Julia his lover and fellow-musician as his passport. Like John in *The Golden Gate*, Michael remains lonely, insecure and alienated and therefore, self-centred, possessive and demanding in relationships. Like John with Liz Dorati, Michael, for all his passionate love for Julia, batters again and again at her fragile sensibilities. Julia, now almost totally deaf, withdraws from ensemble playing into a world of dazzling solo performances and returns to her marriage and her child, substituting passion for security. Liz plunges into a stable but loveless marriage with Phil. Both John and Michael are given to black moods of depression, which make stability impossible. Unlike Philip, Michael has no way of proving himself against dictatorial authority, despite his enormous talent. He feels his sense of inferiority, his working class origin closing in upon him at every challenge and taunt issued to him, like a tinnitus in the brain. His brain refuses to obey the notes before him, his fingers stumble upon his beloved Tononi violin: 'I feel as if I am in two worlds. . . . Somewhere I sense a door closing on me. The sounds merge: customers in several languages, frozen turkeys silent in a morgue, the whirring of the motor that runs the meat fridge, a desperate need to escape from everything around me.'[7]

With Julia re-entering his life as a lover and a soul-mate in music, Michael begins to re-experience the world around him through its multitude of sounds only because his Julia cannot. What she is bravely struggling to come to terms with, he cannot endure and this intensifies his despair. The contrast between his own working class background and that of Julia's American banker-husband, accentuates the crisis. Michael's breakdown and breakaway from his beloved Maggiore quartet is as much an identity crisis as a protest against an insensitive world of the culture capitals where neither the talented Julia's deafness nor his own breakdown is forgivable, much less acceptable.

This simultaneous existence in two worlds is the eternal bane of exiles and expatriates the much-travelled Seth seems to say, if indeed these nomenclatures have not lost their validity. John, with powerful memories of a traumatic childhood, remains a perpetual refugee, having lost both friend and lover. Essentially lonely and insecure himself, he cannot compromise his fixed beliefs and shuttered vision, which are his only fortresses. One way of defending one's imperilled identity is by defining oneself as what others are not, in opposition to the other. Like Pushkin's hero whose 'virulence that made you smile/ his epigrams topped up with bile.' (*EO* I lxvi) John does not like his totems shaken. He is openly derisive of Phil and the Peaceniks' proposed demonstration against Lungless Labs, the heart of America's missile programme, accusing them of high treason at the height of the Cold War. He is disgusted and horrified that his best friend Phil and Ed, Liz's brother, are lovers and generally suffers from what the author calls the ostrich syndrome. Bi-sexuality like Phil's or Seth's own, homosexual relations as those between Piers and Alex or Tobias in *An Equal Music*, or Phil and Ed are symptoms of deviation from the norm, further heightening the theme of alienation, particularly since Ed suffers from an overwhelming sense of guilt due to his Christian upbringing. This does not allow him any satisfaction within the relationship itself and alienates him from Phil, his Jewish lover as well. Relationships fracture easily in the city that itself rests upon a fractured tectonic plate, the San Andreas Fault. Phil and Claire drift apart, divorced by religious and class differences tragically causing little Paul to forfeit his motherland. Phil and Ed have ferocious quarrels splintered again by religion. John and Jan join, break away and then join again only to be tragically severed by death. Liz and John separate, prised apart by differences of viewpoint and John's shuttered outlook upon the world and his refusal to compromise. The city of St. Francis, saint of compassion, shows no compunction in rejecting the lonely and alienated.

The metropolis, recognized as the culture capital of Europe as in *An Equal Music* or the city of vastly enhanced opportunities in America as in *The Golden Gate,* is nevertheless cold, forbidding and indifferent. Malcolm Bradbury, talking of the paradoxical effect of big city culture upon the sensitive individual earlier on in the century, had said:

> In these cities, with their cafes and cabarets, magazines, publishers and galleries, the new aesthetics were distilled; generations argued, and movements contested; the new causes and forms became matters of struggle and campaign. . . . They were mostly cities with a well-established humanistic role, traditional cultural and artistic centres, places of art, learning and ideas. But they were also often novel, carrying within themselves the complexity and tension of modern metropolitan life, which so deeply underlies modern consciousness and modern writing.[8]

The city-poem or city-novel is the most favoured form in Modernist writing, says Bradbury, and Seth exploits both to their utmost bringing out the inner life of cities which houses some of the most painful and bewildering contradictions. While *The Golden Gate* deals with busy San Francisco harbouring such oppositions as Lungless Labs and Peace Marches, tectonic faults and the benediction of the bridge that heals, *An Equal Music* is a tale of three cities, capitals of culture in their own way, London, Vienna and Venice, home to the arts and architecture, Western classical music and the opera. While Seth may not be quite as severe on his cities as Bradbury, who further talks of the 'cultural chaos bred by the populous ever-growing city, a contingent and polyglot Tower of Babel,'[9] his San Francisco, London or Vienna can be quite as ruthless and unforgiving towards the lapses of an upcoming artist struggling to keep his head above water. Piers in *An Equal Music*, flits from auction to auction for a good violin where non-musicians bid higher and higher to put the much-coveted instrument out of his reach, taking his bread and butter away from him. Michael, in the same novel, teeters on the brink of a law suit to keep his beloved Tononi violin out of the reach of avaricious beneficiaries of his mentor's estate. Janet Hayakawa in *The Golden Gate* fights to keep sanity at bay as critics and art journals lambast her work, like trendy and senile worms with their hearts in soup cans and bat dung. Janus-faced, the same critics raise her to Parnassian heights when she dies in a tragic car accident. We are reminded of Seth's poem, *The Frog and the Nightingale* where the frog presiding over Bingle Bog and editor of *The Bog Trumpet*, takes the melody out of the nightingale's voice and literally hounds her to death. Ironically, the big city closes over with indifference to the tragedy in rush hour Frisco in which Jan, Joan and Matt are mowed down by an alcoholic teenager and little Chuck abruptly orphaned. The case is dismissed in favour of the teenager on grounds of his youth. No ripples tell of the lives that have been snuffed out before their time. Michael, who calls London his city, though only by virtue of naturalization, says to Julia in *An Equal Music*, 'Do you remember how I used to unwind as soon as I got out of the city?' (180)

City life suffocates him, he lives high up in Archangel Court in an eerie-like apartment. Disappointed on all fronts, he seeks to drown his alienation in the icy Serpentine with the Water Serpents, taking on impossible tasks to invigorate his tired body. To John in *The Golden Gate,* lonely and unloved, the material quality of big city life is represented by a Porsche-caged blonde, one night stands with cute chicks at the Winking Owl Bar and the anonymity of jobs where conscience can be shrugged away at will.

San Francisco is also represented in miniature by the Peacenik demonstration, a synthesis of races and creeds, norms and exceptions, makers of war and makers of peace, bi-sexuals and homosexuals, pulpitless preachers and colourful demonstrators on stilts, inflated blue rubber whales, exotic pets and cats in prams—all representative of the freedom of speech, the cultural imperialism and arrogant flamboyance of the greatest power on earth. As Bruce King comments: 'Seth's celebration of San Francisco, travel, cosmopolitan pleasures and American comforts has a dual function. It wards off loneliness, the continuing consciousness of having left home, and it creates an exciting, sophisticated world to replace what has been lost.' (230)

A city's shapes to Seth are states of mind, containing certain indelible landmarks that assume the vastness and impregnability of monuments in an individual's memory. When they go, the sense of belonging goes too, and only the sense of a failed homecoming remains. Seth however, is insistent on atmosphere and states of mind, sketching details of scenery, seasonal variations, flowers, fragrances, the call of birds, the coming of Spring, the autumnal flamboyance with a Keatsian fullness and sensuality. London, in *An Equal Music* is not just Oxford Street where people greet each other from the tops of double-decker buses, it is also the Park, the tickle of ice floes on the Serpentine, the honking of the migrating geese, the first reddish twigs and leaves on the lime bush in Spring and the swans on the pond. And though San Francisco in *The Golden Gate* is a city that fractures relationships, resting as it does on a fractured tectonic plate, above all of this presides the Bay, daughter of the Pacific. The history of the Golden Gate bridge itself embodies the paradox underlying Seth's image of the city. On the first anniversary of the Great Earthquake of 1906, Eliza A. Pittsinger wrote in *A Poem of the Earthquake:*

It was the Great Iconoclast
Whose deadly grip and fiery blast
Awoke the world to pity.
San Francisco drained the cup—
But she is bravely waking up.[10]

And so the story of the city is not only the saga of fractured relationships but of the healing benediction of the great Golden Gate that presides like a colossus over the novel. The bridge, known till 1937 as 'the bridge that couldn't be built,' is a testimony of man's courageous struggle to combat the fury of Nature. During the years of the Great Depression, engineers braved persistent foggy weather, sixty miles per hour winds and strong ocean currents that whipped through a deep canyon below, to complete it:

> A deliquescent wash of blue
> Reveals the bridge, long lost to view
> In summer's quilt of fog: the towers,
> High-built, red-gold, with their long span
> —The most majestic spun by man. (*GG* 9.28)

Ed goes to the Golden Gate in all his loneliness by night and feels a benediction stealing over his heart. The bridge invites Liz and Phil to re-think their lives after a period of bitter disillusionment, to reject the storms of passion in favour of calm and stability, to build a home and shelter the homeless, to give up the ostrich syndrome and broaden their outlook upon the world. John, walking along the bridge with Jan, watches the whales come home in pods and pairs, overcomes his cynical hatred of Liz and Phil and dreams of a home for himself and Jan. Jan finds here a perfect sand dollar, a 'seal of oceanic power'[19] which reminds her of her grandmother's courageous struggle to survive against dire adversity. The recovery of this token after Jan's tragic death brings John back to the human fold again. He is touched by the healing grace of the great bridge that towers over their lives.

The suburban who ventures out in search of better pastures to the metropolis and the culture-capitals, has left behind him the unbroken continuity of generations within which he is rooted, the bond of traditions and customs—in short, all that a home can mean to an exile. Liz and Ed in competitive careers in San Francisco and Sue about to launch herself in Paris, have left behind them the rock-solid foundation of family. It is a family rooted in the soil and in hard labour in the family vineyard. These are people whom the vagaries of land and weather have seasoned to face adversity with stoic calm. At a family gathering at Thanksgiving at Sonata County, discovering the old documents in the attic is like re-building the family tree. The Thanksgiving lunch, the parents' wistful longing for the children to settle down with marriage and babies are all part of the desire for continuity. It is like Michael's ritual Christmas lunch, the dinner at Owd Bett with father and aunt and the song of the larks in the hollow on the muirs in Rochedale in *An Equal Music*. Vine pruning as a ritualistic activity has a calming and sobering influence on John too, just as Mrs. Craven's olive-picking and pickling does. The year moves on, the seasons pass, the back-breaking demands of grape harvesting helps Liz's father overcome the trauma of his wife's death. It provides a rich and hallowed contrast to the stark impersonality of Jan's untimely death in the cold aloneness of a big city hospital room, bereft of her loved ones. The death of Liz's mother is almost simultaneous with the birth of Liz's son, keeping unbroken the continuity, 'intertwining / Their lives along a common vine.' (*GG* 10.24) Liz and Phil together build a home, which gives shelter to other homeless and orphaned. In *Two Lives*, Vikram Seth is himself overcome by a longing for home back in India, to indulge in all the many activities as a son and as a brother to Aradhana. Often he is content to find a substitute home with Shanti Uncle and Henny, his German Jewish aunt, who give him shelter with memories of Henny's own destroyed home in Nazi Germany. In *An Equal Music*, the de-facing of Rochedale, the substitution of the family butcher's shop by a car park, may symbolize the tragic end of an era, but it is where Michael, defeated by the deafening challenges of big city life, dreams of sanctuary. Lying in the hollow on the muirs, sheltered from the sloughing winds, he hears the larks ascending and their song high up in the sky. Michael as a musician can identify with the lark's song. Like the lark, Michael wishes to make his own music beyond the dictates of critics and recording companies, fanfare, publicity and launches, all of which Seth satirizes in his poem *The Hare and the Tortoise*,

Soon she saw her name in lights,
Sold a book and movie rights,
While a travel magazine
Bought the story, sight unseen
Of her three hour expedition
To the wood.[11]

Michael wishes to move beyond public acclaim or disdain, beyond even the collective identity of the quartet and the challenge of Julia in 'The Art of Fugue.' 'Now two, now three, and now, though the sky is scarcely brighter, legions of larks rise up from the damp earth in careless counterpoint, each retaining its self even as it merges with its fellows. But why can't the lark not be itself alone, uninvested, uncompared, even by those who love it most?' (*EM* 319)

Michael has eventually re-defined his own identity through storm and stress and is on the way to finding harbour, just as John, with Jan's precious sand dollar in his hand, looks forward to the fold that has stretched out its arms to receive its prodigal son. While defining oneself in contradistinction to 'the other' is a way of fighting alienation, the search for cultural roots and connections is instinctive and one's best defence against the crisis of identity that overcomes one in a clash of cultures along 'fault lines' which Huntington speaks of and Seth highlights through his tectonic metaphor of the San Andreas Fault.

NOTES

1. Salman Rushdie, *Imaginary Homelands* (Granta Books in association with Penguin India, 1991), p. 10.
2. Samuel P. Huntington, *The Clash of Civilizations and the Remaking of World Order* (Penguin, New Delhi, 1997), p. 125.
3. Vikram Seth, *The Golden Gate* (Penguin with Faber and Faber, New Delhi, 1986), p. 260, 11.53.
4. Bruce King, *Modern Indian Poetry in English* (Oxford University Press, New Delhi, 1987), p. 214.
5. Vikram Seth, *The Humble Administrator's Garden* qtd. *Modern Indian Poetry in English*, Bruce King, p. 12.

6. A.S. Pushkin, *Eugene Onegin* trans. Charles H. Johnston (Penguin, England, 1979), p. 52, I. xxxviii.
7. Vikram Seth, *An Equal Music* (Viking, Penguin, New Delhi, 1999), p.179.
8. Malcolm Bradbury and James McFarlane, ed., *Modernism: A Guide to European Literature (1890-1930)* (Penguin, England, 1976), p. 97.
9. *Ibid.*, pp. 98-99.
10. Eliza A. Pittsinger, *A Poem of the Earthquake* in *American Women: Fifteen Hundred Biographies*, Francis E. Willard and Mary A. Livermore, ed., Cromwell and Kirkpatrick (1893; revised ed., 1987) p.573.
11. Vikram Seth, *Beastly Tales from Here and There* (Viking, Penguin, New Delhi, 1991), p. 40.

The Golden Gate and *A Suitable Boy* as Expatriate Novels

SANDHYA RAO MEHTA

With the crossing over to a distant land of ostensible opportunity and potential prosperity, the Indian expatriate comes face-to-face with unimaginable problems and situations, not least of all those manifested in the cruel weather conditions of the Canadian winter. The freezing temperatures in Northern Canada as well as the sheer distance of the California act as metaphorical realities to express the cold and distant reception which awaited the Indian immigrant to Canada and the United States throughout the twentieth century. Expatriation and displacement, never very comfortable experiences, are further underlined with a sense of despondency, bringing in its wake powerful notions of marginalization, dispossession and a final dismissal as the 'other' from the dominant community.

The poetry of these expatriates is also helpful in exploring the varying facets of expatriate experience. The poetry is distinctly laced with detachment, irony and often nostalgia for lost experiences and possibilities. While groping with the twin worlds merging in the centre of poetic experience, Indian poets like A.K. Ramanujan and Shiv Kumar create, not so much a distinct community but project themselves as enmeshed between cultures. Thus Ramanujan speaks in a detached fashion of his mother whose last image is contained within the framework of daily ritual:

> Mother's farewell had no words,
> no tears, only a long look
> that moved on your body

from top to toe
with the advice that you should
not forget your oil bath
every Tuesday
when you go to America.[1]

Vikram Seth assertively vocalizes the futility of placing identities within a time and space specific context:

The world is a bridge. Pass over it
Building no house upon it
Acceptance may come with time
Rest then, disquieted heart.[2]

Memory, and thus a deliberately cultivated sense of identity, becomes the hallmark of Indian expatriate poetry.

Vikram Seth earns a mention as an expatriate Indian, although not strictly one in the limited definition of the term, by various listings of prominent South Asian Americans amongst whom he is commonly included. In fact, *Notable Asian Americans*, published in 1996, refers to Bharati Mukherjee, Vikram Seth, Bapsi Sidhwa and Amitav Ghosh as the most prominent South Asian American novelists.[3] Thus labelled, Seth inevitably belongs to the parameters of American expatriate writing, however reluctantly.[4] This reluctance is best reflected in his own works which doggedly avoid confrontational issues of hybridity and marginalization to seemingly reactionary images of modernistic yuppie life in California.

The Golden Gate, Seth's epic fiction in verse, borrows modernism's assumptions of ennui and purposelessness into the context of American upper middle class. The novel has been praised for being able to "deconstruct the canonic models with a view to question, expose and dismantle the underlining structures and question the imperialist assumptions."[5] Such a critical ambition proves more than the efforts which this fiction actually allows. By adopting the sonnet form, Seth succeeds in showing the gap between romantic, courtly assumptions and culture behind the form against the dull, dry and highly practical life of the yuppies rather than "interrogate the socio-cultural assumptions entailed in the sonnet form."[6] By dwelling on broken relationships, homosexuality, advertised courtships and nuclear threats in "San Francisco's restless history,"[7] Seth is firmly rooting his fictive negative in the western world and the ways of his adopted land rather than catapulting it in any manner into the Indian context. Phrases like "love is the friction/Of two skins" (52) and "love's a mere word" (266) belong solely to the modern world of cosmopolitan America with little relevance to his homeland.

Stylistically innovative and narratively engrossing, *The Golden Gate*, however, offers little in terms of exploration of the postmodern condition of totality and absorption of all experience. If, as Aijaz Ahmed, quoting Lyotard states that "postmodernism is a set of tendencies within late Modernism itself which distinguishes itself primarily by celebrating human inability to experience reality as a totality over and beyond its fragments," (Ahmed, 218) *The Golden Gate* appears to remain a testament to the modernist sentiments which stress the predominance of valueless relationships, of the absurd ennui of contemporary existence in which "A linkless node, no spouse or sibling, No children/ John wanders alone into an ice cream parlor." (6) That angst is a predominant state of being in this narrative is evident in the almost existential journey of John who walks into a parlour alone and is finally left as "he tries to wring meaning from things that have no meaning." (294) This meaninglessness of contemporary existence is, however, limited within the framework of American society as there are few indications of its being a predicament of the general human condition.

The Golden Gate appears in the field of experimentation as the most dramatic of all fictions written by Indian expatriate writers composed in the form of a sonnet in tetrameters reminiscent of both Dante and Pushkin. The novel has as its central theme, the solitariness of American Yuppiedom. Innovative and even delightfully moving, *The Golden Gate* has little beyond the sheer novelty of form to commend it. Form and theme are related, as the form of a narrative must largely be indicative of the central concerns of a creative work. In this case, however; the innovativeness of the sonnet form brings with it, neither the sense of a lost world, nor the promise of an idyllic existence of Dantean proportions, but serves merely to focus upon the nullity, absurd dilemma and absence of values in a moral world. A fusion of word and meaning is missing in this novel-in-verse which ostensibly deals with the existential condition of man who "caught in the kelp of loneliness, cries for help." (4) Throughout this reading, there is a sense of the ingenuity of the writer drawing attention upon himself, rather than to the existential angst-ridden condition of his protagonist. Seth defends his chosen form as an attempt to raise it over the mere 'hudibrastic tricks' to which it has descended but much of Seth's own verse appears to achieve little else. In this respect, the novel remains trite, innovative but extremely self-conscious. Alan Hollinghurst speaks of Seth's virtuosity in *The Golden Gate* lacking a soul and a purpose and concludes that "it is very hard in the end to state what one thinks of this book except that such sharp-eyed and sophisticated talent can go on to do something even more extraordinary; perhaps something which strikes more unhesitatingly to the heart of the matter."[8]

If *The Golden Gate* escapes being defined as Indian fiction owing largely to its firm American locale, Seth's next novel, a 1400 page tale of social realism *A Suitable Boy* establishes Seth, not as an Indian expatriate but an artist interested in the affairs of India. Highly praised and compared to Tolstoy's and Dickens' fiction, *A Suitable Boy* has none of the sweep, philosophical grasp or permanent truths of human nature that underline these epic narratives in the history of the novel. Seth uses the setting of postcolonial India but the humour and the layers of irony implicit in the novel deny a sense of the imaginative quest and creative tussle with which the Indian expatriate exile is so characterized. The concerns of language, style, presentation and technique are absent as the novel consciously emulates the great tradition of the mainstream English novel from Fielding to Hardy. In fact, as noted academic and critic C.D Narasimhaiah comments, Seth has achieved little in this novel except to display his "infinite patience to observe trivia in upper class Indian society and record it meticulously, to what end, only he can tell."[9]

Whether *A Suitable Boy* strikes the heart or not, it remains a resounding work of tremendous topical import primarily owing to the media hype about the work prior to release. Not strictly an expatriate work,[10] *A Suitable Boy* automatically belongs to a category of historical fiction seeking to re-create a specific period of Indian history through a range of characters with varying degrees of involvement to the central action. Gita Mehta's *Raj* which shall be discussed later may be viewed in the same category.

A Suitable Boy opens with the marriage of Savita, Mr. Pran Mehra's daughter His other daughter Lata's quest for the ideal husband as well as her brother-in-law Maan's search for a meaningful vocation in life provides the thread of the plot in *A Suitable Boy.* Around these predominant themes revolve the diverse aspects of a growing India preparing for its first general election after independence. The passing of a new law abolishing the zamindari system and the inevitable Indian realities of famines, floods and kumbh melas create the daily rituals of a changing, yet eternal India. For all its range of characters, action and themes, however, what *A Suitable Boy* lacks is the depth of vision which moves. It is an accusation to which Seth, in spite of his protests of not being an outsider, necessarily succumbs, for the picture of the 1950s India portrayed in the novel is superficial and at best, patronizing. It is a gentle tale which wears the reader away from the cruel realities of life, where people survive riots, famines, even a stampede at the kumbh mela from which a ten-year-old Bhaskar is rescued. The Hindu-Muslim riots over the presence of a mosque gather momentum, but the characters are lucky enough to conclude the incident without too many casualties:

> The District Magistrate looked around at his men. A couple of them were trembling, most of them were jubilant. None of them was injured. He caught the head constable's eye. Both of them started laughing with relief, then stopped. A couple of women were waiting in nearby houses. Otherwise, everything was peaceful, rather, still.[11]

Lata's final choice of reason over passion and indeed her deliberate rejection of the life of passion represented by Kabir points to an attitude with which the novel is surfeit. Love, passion and sexual power appear to be sacrifices necessitated by the compulsions of everyday existence where the imperatives of loyalty and continuity remain of paramount import. This is how Lata justifies her decision to marry Harish: "Look at what passion has done to the family. Maan's broken, his mother's dead, his father's in despair. When I thought that Kabir was seeing someone else, what I remember feeling was enough to make me hate passion." (1296)

A Suitable Boy may ultimately bear images of a gentle India swaying daily through the patterns of a monotonous routine, but the predominant picture which emerges is of a contained world of Edenic qualities, where decisions have few consequences beyond one's immediate surroundings, families care little beyond the tinkle of rich crystal and success and happiness is measured in terms of one's capacity to marry the right person. The novel may be known for its "uneventfulness, its surpassing dailiness, the way in which Seth caught a life sized human, unextraordinary India,"[12] yet the picture created remains an outsider's vision of India, one for whom the traumatic and cataclysmic consequences of political action retain only their theoretic import. The political predilections too are dismissed without much aplomb for the repercussion on the common man even on issues like prostitution and feudalism are dealt in equally asinine fashion:

> As he washed his hands, Mahesh Kapoor thought about his old friend, the Nawab of Bailar. He would be one of those most deeply affected by the passage of the zamindari Abolition Bill. . . . If the lifestyle of a good few men like the Nawab sahib had to be sacri-

> ficed for the greater good of millions of tenant farmers, it was a cost that had to be borne. (264)

Critics at various points of their discussion of *The Golden Gate* and *A Suitable Boy* commend Seth's works for the distance and perspective which characterize the delineation of plot and character. Marjorie Perloff, in fact, states in the *American Poetry Review* that "As an Indian, educated at Oxford and hence having the vantage point of the outsiders' witness on the California scene, Vikram Seth has been praised all around for his sharp eye for social nuances,"[13] yet it is this distance, the presentation of which remains the glaring drawback in *A Suitable Boy*. The novel contains political intrigue and layers of social relationships all enmeshed in an interconnected fashion which is so characteristic of Indian society. Yet there is a way in which the novel lacks the predominant emotion of involvement. Much attention is given to details: "She moved the pallu of her silk saree further forward over her head; it tended to slip down and one of her most charming gestures—to be repeated throughout the evening—was to adjust her sari to ensure that her head was not left uncovered." (79) Yet, the scene remains a gesture, almost a type of the courtesan who belongs to any place or time rather than being firmly entrenched in the social realities of the 1950s India. The cocktail conversations at Arun's house in Calcutta abound in the inanities with which the characters and plot swerve in the same detached and ironic tone with which the novelist treats all his characters:

> As she prattled on and on Lata looked at her wonderingly. Of course, every girl in the family learns these things at an early age. For the first time Patricia Cox looked less than completely bored. But by the time the souffle came around, she had lapsed into passivity. (996)

NOTES

1. Vikram Seth, *The Poems* (New Delhi: Penguin, 1995), p. 13.

2. *Ibid.*
3. Vikram Seth, in an interview with Michele Field states that he may not have been considered the best, young Indian artist if he had stayed on in California, "but now they will have to." Michele Field, "Vikram Seth," *Publishers Weekly*, Vol. 240, No. 19 (May 10,1993), p. 47.
4. David Myers, "Vikram Seth's Epic Renunciation of the Passions: Deconstructing Moral Codes in *A Suitable Boy," Fiction of the Nineties*, p. 73.
5. Supriya Karunakaran, "'Games the Novelists Play': The Rebellion of Vikram Seth in *The Golden Gate* and Shashi Tharoor in *The Great Indian Novel," Fiction of the Nineties*, p. 96.
6. Vikram Seth, *The Golden Gate* (New Delhi: Penguin, 1986), p. 52.
7. Allan Hollinghurst "In the Onegin Line," *The Times Literary Supplement*, No. 43-44 (July 4, 1986), p. 733.
8. C.D. Narasimhaiah "Spurious Reputations: Vikram Seth, Salman Rushdie, Shashi Tharoor," *Essays in Commonwealth Literature* (Delhi: Pencraff International, 1995), p. 122.
9. *A Suitable Boy* was written over a six-year period in which the novelist stayed at his parents' house in Calcutta.
10. Vikram Seth, *A Suitable Boy* (London: Viking, 1993), p. 238.
11. Pica Iyer, "India *day-by-day," Times Literary Supplement*, No. 4694 (March 19,1993), p. 20.
12. Marjorie Perloff, "'Homeward Ho!': Silicon Valley Pushkin," *The American Poetry Review*, Vol. 16, No. 6 (Nov.-Dec. 1986), pp. 37-46.

The Horizon of Vikram Seth's Fiction

GOPARANJAN MISRA
S.B.R. Govt. Women's College, Berhampur

Vikram Seth, a student of Economics, while writing a doctoral dissertation at the Stanford University, U.S.A. got interested in poetry which eventually led him to write a novel in verse. The publication of *The Golden Gate* had been preceded by two other books: *From Heaven Lake*—an account of Seth's travels in China—and *The Humble Administrator's Garden*, a book of verse. But it is the novel which brought him immediate recognition. It has been very favourably reviewed by many leading critics. John Hollander calls it "a brilliantly fashioned" tale of life among a number of Bay area "Yuppies" and that it is "never anything less than quaintly and most unqualifiedly marvellous."[1] X.J. Kennedy admires its "fluency"[2] and M. Perloff quotes Susan Sontag who compares it to Pushkin's *Eugene Onegin* in its "particular mix of wit, sagacity and rue" and praises it as a "thrilling, subtle literary achievement."[3]

The Golden Gate deals with the common human search for love, affection and sense of belonging. Dejection and an acute sense of loneliness are the experiences of most of the characters in the novel and they wander about, seeking meaning and emotional fulfilment. Seth strives to give a realistic portrayal of the life these characters live and the society to which they belong.

Twenty-six-year-old John is a gray-eyed, blond-haired, aristocratic handsome young man working as a successful Silicon Valley executive. His corporate stock is booming. He has an abnormal appetite for work, and apparently there is nothing wrong around him that should upset him. But he seems to be overwhelmed with grief. An acute feeling of loneliness grips him and he wonders if anyone would miss him in case he died suddenly. He feels 'a cold cast of self-pity envelop him.'[4] As such he is living alone. His mother is dead, his English father, retired in his native Kent, rarely responds to his letters. He looks around. There seems to be life and fun everywhere. The sights of a pair of giggling lovers, frolicking school girls, a clamorous family adds to his misery. He grows disconsolate and realizes the inadequacy of either money or drugs in alleviating one's sorrows. He murmurs:

> Money—it's a gas!
> The lunatic is on the grass. (7)

He 'senses his life has run to seed' (5) for 'No family cushions his solitude.' (6) He tries to contact a few friends over phone but fails and while he engages himself in 'pensive prose' like Hardy's *Life's Little Ironies*, Donne's gloomier sermons and *The Zibaldone of Leopardi*, an ex-lover, Janet Hakawa calls back and listens sympathetically to his problems:

> Jan, I don't know what's wrong
> I'm young, employed, healthy, ambitious
> Sound, solvent, self-made, self-possessed
> But all my symptoms are pernicious.
> . . . The sunflower of my youth is wilting
> The tower of my dreams is tilting
> The zoom lens of my zest is blurred
> The drama of my life's absurd
> What is the root of my neurosis?
> I jog, eat brewer's yeast each day
> And yet I feel life slip away
> I wait your sapient diagnosis.
> I die! I faint! I fall! I sink!

To this Janet replies: "You need a lover, John, I think" (14) and playfully puts an advertisement in the newspaper, in the hope of procuring a partner for John who initially gets annoyed at the idea but subsequently grows curious as he goes through the responses. He meets one Elisabeth Dorati (Liz)—a young, buxom, intelligent lawyer and they become friends. They meet in the park, restaurants and at musical concerts, invariably occupying themselves in sweet babbles like moonstruck lovers do. But as they enjoy greater physical proximity, they fall out with each other. The initial spurts of amorous fervour get dampened as they discover that they are temperamentally incompatible. They quarrel over trifles (like a pet dog) and finally break off their engagement. Other characters like Ed, Liz's younger brother, Phil Weiss, John's school chum are introduced and are said to read Proust, St. Thomas Acquinas, Zen philosophy but their main concerns are the problems of loneliness. Meanwhile Phil and Ed are attracted to a homosexual relationship. Ed feels guilty as the Bible condemns such relations:

> The Bible says, if a man lie
> With a man, he must surely die. (97)

Phil is not convinced and argues:

> That old book, Ed holds plenty of rules
> That may have made sense once. (97)

And goes on to say that God would not grudge such relation. However, they stand opposed to each other, lapse into bitter silence, shake hands and turn away.

Meanwhile Liz learns of her mother's illness which is critical and keeping in mind the latter's wish to see a grandchild, marries Phil. This marriage is, however, less prompted by passion than maturity. Both of them have realized from their personal experience that passion does not contribute to lasting relationship. Phil says:

> Passion's prelude to disaster
> It's something else that makes me sure
> Our bond can last five decades more. (244)

And Liz echoes the same sentiments:

> And I'd far rather

Marry a man who's a good father
Than someone. . . . I too don't feel sure
I can trust passion any more. (245)

In these lines Seth anticipates the theme of renunciation of passion that he takes up in his *A Suitable Boy* in greater details and intensity.

John feels greatly humiliated by the marriage between Liz and Phil and Janet's attempt at reconciliation proves futile. Liz and Phil give importance to parenthood and gradually take charge of three children: Phil's son, Paul, by his first marriage, little Chuck Lamont, the son of their friends who meet their sudden end in an accident, and their own child whom they call John. Janet dies and John is thrown to utter despair. He feels he would never regain the 'fervour to outlive this pain.' His 'despair-demented brain' is haunted by a guilt feeling that he had played a part in Janet's death. Overwhelmed with grief he recalls every trifle, every commonplace incident associated with her and thus broods over the past. He can hear her voice calling him. Disconsolate, he wanders rather aimlessly.

In the meantime, Phil and Liz are blessed with a son and Liz's ailing mother breathes her last. They can now realize John's anguish better and they write a letter inviting him to join them. John opens it and, rather hesitantly, goes through it. The contents of the letter make him charged with emotion and his eyes are filled with tears. The letter reads:

Dear John, we have a son,
We hope that you'll be his godfather
We have called him John . . .
Please speak to us, John. In the end,
We'll all be old or dead or dying,
My mother died two weeks ago . . .
Phil and I send our love.
Liz (306)

The novel ends with a much more matured John, trying to share his thoughts and feelings with others to lessen his agony, instead of indulging in self-pity as we find him in the opening stanzas,

Thus we find in the novel all the characters craving for love and affection, the inadequacy of material prosperity to assuage an individual's sense of loneliness and the resultant agony. While presenting a wide sweep of social life, Seth vividly evokes the sights, sounds and typical life rhythms of the city of San Francisco. We get a feel of the atmosphere that prevails at various places like parks, beaches, restaurants, theatres and other public places. There are tongue-in-the-cheek remarks about critics whose criticism is motivated by factors other than that which should concern them. Seth gives air to his views on love and marriage. He seems to have a conviction that youthful love and mutual attraction do not form the basis of a happy, long-lasting married life which requires for its success a deeper understanding of each other on the part of the partners and a willingness to accommodate each other's interests. The author deals with other areas like the contrast between the world of the children and that of the grown-ups, the animals that fascinate and repel human beings, the environmental pollution and Anti-Nuclear War.

But the novel "primarily reflects a concern with the fleeting nature of youth, passion of life and how one must snatch some significant relationship of love and understanding to make it an anchor of one's life."[5]

Seth,'s 'quietly monumental' first prose novel *A Suitable Boy*[6] apparently deals with a simple theme of quest for a suitable boy on the part of Rupa Mehra, the materfamilias of the Mehra family, for her younger daughter Lata, who is "nineteen years old, brilliant at her studies, came first in her Senior Cambridge exams from Sophia Convent, did her Intermediate Arts from Brahmpur University and has just finished (with excellent marks) her first B.A. exams in English. She is 5 ft.5 in. tall, not very fair, but attractive and smart in an Indian sort of way."

(566) This is how Kalpana describes Lata in her letter to Haresh, the prospective suitable boy of the novel.

Lata has three suitors among whom she has to choose one as her life-partner—Kabir Durrani, Amit Chatterjee and Haresh Khanna. Seth takes pains to write in detail about her affairs with each one of them so that they can be judged dispassionately and the final choice be justified. Lata's encounter with Kabir throws her into a kind of euphoria. His nearly six feet athletic frame, wheatish complexion, an aquiline nose and black wavy hair captivates her. Seized with passion, she exclaims: "I'm behaving like a fascinated gopi—soon, instead of feeling jealous of Krishna's flute I'll start envying Kabir's bat." (147) She asks him his name, on meeting him for the third time and the young man's face breaks into a happy grin:

> 'Ah!' he said, 'I thought you would never ask. I'm Kabir, but very recently my friends have started calling me Galahad.'
>
> 'Why?'
>
> 'Because they think that I spend my time rescuing damsels in distress.' (146)

But the irony of the situation is that, at present, he is throwing a damsel into distress. She finds out that he is a Muslim and that this amorous relation will not lead to marriage as her family will be dead against him. She is further advised to 'always find out the last name of any one with an ambiguous first name.' In fact when Rupa Mehra learns of the affair, she becomes furious and is shocked by the surname of Lata's lover. The three deadly syllables (Durrani) have their effect. She clutches at her heart, opens her mouth in silent horror, looks unseeingly around the room and asks:

> 'Do you want to marry him.'
>
> 'Yes!'
>
> 'He'll marry you—and next year he'll say "Talaq talaq talaq" and you'll be out on the streets. You obstinate girl.' (182)

But Lata has a strange will of her own. She does not give in easily. Quiet but unpredictable, 'though named after that most pliable thing, a vine, which was trained to cling,' she strongly reminds her mother of what father had told them—that 'we should follow our own hearts.' But she is destined to get disillusioned soon, for while she is prepared to do anything for love—elope and get married—she finds Kabir falter.

His explanation that he has to build his career first is unconvincing for the impassioned Lata who feels heartbroken and humiliated. Besides, he does not know how he would overcome the impracticality of an inter-racial marriage in India of 1951. Later, of course, she tells her best friend Malti why she has renounced her romantic infatuation with the Muslim Kabir Durrani: "I am not myself when I'm with him. I ask myself who is this—this jealous obsessed woman who can't get a man out of her head—why should I make myself suffer like this? I know that it will always be like this if I'm with him." (1296)

The talented but eccentric, self-indulgent poet Amit Chatterjee from Calcutta is rejected by Lata because in his total dedication to his Muse, he does not really need her. Besides, he seems ill-equipped to shoulder mundane, marital responsibilities in the long run.

Haresh Khanna, a product of St. Stephen's college, working for CLFC (Cawnpore Leather & Footwear Company), a teetotaler, seems to be ideologically acceptable to Seth and his female protagonist Lata, since he is egalitarian, hard-working, honest, outspoken, in need of a marital partner and will agree to Lata pursuing an independent career as a teacher. All these qualities amply compensate his brashness in society. Lata speaks to Malti about him: "Haresh is practical, he's forceful, he isn't cynical. He gets things done and he helps people without making a fuss about it." (1297) "Haresh's feet touch the ground, and he has dust and sweat and a shadow. The other two are a bit too God-like and ethereal to be any good for me." (1299)

The very beginning of the novel with Rupa Mehra speaking to Lata 'You too will marry a boy I choose' states Seth's thematic concern, but the novel is about far more than a nubile, middle-class girl indulging in the luxury of choosing a husband. So many varied themes like religious frenzy and communal disharmony, higher education, attempt to transform political power structure through the First General Election, the plight of artists, musicians and courtesans like Saeeda Bai who face the loss of patronage with the abolition of the Zamindari system, have been interwoven to this story of matrimonial alliance. Different aspects of love like romance, lust, extra-marital relation have been dealt with in the novel. Issue of minorities, misery of the untouchables, celebrations of festivals like Holi and Moharram have been realistically portrayed. There are comments on India and Indians in general by English men. The novel contains theories on writing novel. In fact, Seth's first prose novel with its massive bulk (1347 pages and more than 8 lakh words), a host of characters from the four large families—the Mehras, the Kapoors, the Chatterjees and the Khans—and numerous themes interwoven into it, is simply mind-boggling.

To write a novel on such a grand scale with a host of characters and varied incidents, and yet make almost every page of it highly readable—that sounds incredible, but that is a fact. The book has been wrongly accused by some of being diffuse and disjointed since there is 'a close-unit thematic unity to a panoramic epic' as rightly remarked by David Myers.

While reviewing the novel, Rita Joshi comments: "Vikram Seth has indeed created the novel of our times. Immensely readable but deceptively simple, with several layers so that it will evoke different levels of responses in different people. In an age of aggressive intellectualism, Seth has gone back to an older, subtle narrative style of nineteenth century novelists."[7]

For Richard Woodward, the novel is "a saga of modern India."[8] At the heart of it," says Seth about the novel, "it's really a love story." Anita Desai sees Vikram Seth's novel as a comfortable comedy. She says that Seth is "too fond and too tolerant of his characters to want to transform them. Although in their rash youth, they might be tempted by the possibilities of change, defiance, and the unknown, they learn their lessons and return chastened, to the safety and security of the familiar and the traditional, represented here, in the Indian fashion, by the great god family."[9]

Seth with his rare narrative talent supplemented by years of intensive research in collecting necessary details (he took 8 years to write this novel), succeeds in evoking a bygone era with such vividness that the readers are almost transported to those days of young Independent India half a century back. The novel is unique in the sense that it strives to envelop almost all events of all aspects of Indian life in a very short span of period and it is no mean achievement.

After the huge success of *A Suitable Boy*, many of Vikram Seth's admirers as well as critics were apprehensive about his next book, when they learnt that it would deal with the story of a musician. It was understandable since music as the dominant theme has seldom made a mark among the readers, irrespective of the stature of the author. Even Thomas Mann failed with his *Doctor Faustus*. Seth himself had some misgivings and spent moments of indecision before he made up his mind to have a go at it. In his authorial note appended to the novel, he makes it clear: "Music to me is dearer even than speech. When I realised that I would be writing about it I was gripped by anxiety. Only slowly did I reconcile myself to the thought of it."[10] (Music is also the theme of two other contemporary novels—Rushdie's *Ground Beneath her Feet* and Shashi Deshpande's *Small Remedies*).

In fact music pervades the whole of the novel and, admittedly, a knowledge of western classical music will help one towards a better understanding of the work. In it we find music played, performed, recalled, discussed and critically analysed and, a reader, ignorant of the technicalities, is likely to grow impatient and may put the book on the shelf, but if he shows a bit of sympathy for the characters engrossed in a world of music, he will find *An Equal Music* an absorbing novel. John Carey speaks of it in very high terms: "*An Equal Music* is a wonder-work: irresistible, deeply moving . . . it is a novel that can stand being reread and reread, but the first time round it is an emotional cliff-hanger, balanced over nerve-tingling uncertainties."[11]

The story opens in the city of London with a struggling musician, Michael Holme, a 35-year-old violinist from Rochdale, playing with the Maggiore Quartet and giving music lessons to a group of not-so-interested pupils with one of whom he is carrying on a desultory affair. Ten years ago in Vienna, he had fallen in love with a pianist Julia McNicholl. Both of them were students then with Carl Kall as their teacher whom they adored. Carl, a perfectionist, spotted the rich potential in Michael, urged him to persevere uncompromisingly despite the latter's problem. The stress grew unbearable. Michael broke down, fell out with his teacher and, terribly annoyed with Julia for taking the maestro's side, walked out on her.

Back in England, Michael, after a couple of months, regrets his impulsive action, appreciates Julia's stand, and wants to contact her but she seems to have vanished from the face of the earth and thus passes ten years of futile search for her in whose company he has spent brief but ecstatic moments. And finally the long wait comes to an end. Quite accidentally, Michael meets Julia again and all the pent-up passion seems to visit their reunion. But we soon learn that there have been changes in Julia's life. She is married with a seven-year-old son and she is now almost deaf as a result of an illness. They meet secretly. Their love-affair resumes, though "Julia is reluctant to jeopardize her marriage or hurt her husband and child."

They go on a brief tour to Vienna and Venice to perform Schubert's Trout quintet. They borrow a flat in Sant'Elena. The musical and personal stories seem to blend together. In each other's arms they seem to enact a bond that nothing can snap. "But separation looms. Her husband and son await her in London. They can lay claim to her, Michael agonizingly realizes, in ways he cannot." He is left alone only with memories to haunt him.

Into this threadbare plot Seth has packed a number of issues that find an echo in the reader's mind—rift between parents and child regarding choosing a career, agony resulting from being thrown out of one's native place, guilt-feeling associated with extramarital relation, sexual jealousy and, above all, a bitter sense of loneliness that can play havoc with one's life. Seth has been immensely successful in unfolding each emotional intricacy through rare insight and a wonderful narrative style.

The novel, apart from other things, can be read as a turbulent love-story soaked in passion and pathos. Michael's keen interest in music takes him to Vienna and it is here that he meets Julia at a student concert while she is playing Mozart Sonata. They get talking about themselves and discover they are both from England. Seth is at his romantic best when he describes their coming closer to each other: "It was a cold night, with bits of snow and slush on the ground, and Vienna was at its grayest and grimmest. We walked to the restaurant. I slipped, and she stopped me from falling. I kissed her, instinctively—amazed at myself even as I did it—and she was too surprised to object. . . . That winter, that spring, that summer, I lived in a waking dream." (80)

Michael and Julia have lots of differences between them, yet they get drawn to each other. While he has a humble background—his father has a butcher's shop in a small street in Rochdale and no one in their family has ever dreamed of going to university—she has much more sophisticated family background. Her father teaches History at Oxford and she has grown up in an atmosphere of art, literature and music. He realises that she has been brought up in a world "unreachably different from mine." Their love for each other is further intensified by their love for music. Their teacher Carl Kall is quick to spot a rare talent in Michael and secretly nurtures an ambition to see this pupil at the very top and expects him to apply himself to the job with single-hearted devotion. Things move smoothly, but then the whole rhythm is upset when the teacher and the taught rather overreact to an ordinary situation. Michael's third finger begins giving him difficulty. His practice is affected. Carl gets annoyed and urges his student to carry on, and not to attach importance to this negligible factor.

Michael understands the situation but thinks that the teacher is rather unduly harsh and rough on him. He feels aggrieved. Julia defends the teacher's reaction. She is misunderstood. Her defence of Carl appears to Michael an unbearable act of betrayal on her part. He leaves in rage and does not write or call her on phone. Two months go by and when, realizing his mistake, he does write, it remains unanswered.

For ten years Michael carries on a vain search for Julia and then through a series of chance encounters he meets her. The long wait ends, but the situation stands greatly changed. She is married to an American banker from Boston and they have a seven-year-old son, Luke. Besides, she has turned deaf owing to some illness. Michael apologises and tries to revive their old relation but Julia does not encourage his advances since she is reluctant to harm her marriage or hurt her husband and child.

However Julia, despite her gratitude to her husband, cannot, perhaps, forget her old association with Michael. This reunion seems to revive them with all its warmth. They meet surreptitiously and let wild passions overwhelm them: "She kisses me . . . she holds me as if she could never bear to let me desert her again. . . . We make love not with tenderness but with ecstasy born out of starvation. . . . The secret of her body, mixed with her faint perfume drives me into a frenzy." (137)

Michael cannot tolerate Julia's love and longing for her husband. His possessive nature is carried almost to an absurd extent. He is seized with an insane desire to rupture their relation and, the night before Julia leaves for London to join her family, he while making love, in the bitterness of his passion, leaves on her neck and shoulders and arms, bold love-bites. When Julia learns that these bruises have been left on her body intentionally to cause her and her husband embarrassment, she stares at Michael in rage and disbelief. There is mud-slinging from either side and the lovers part. The brief ecstatic moments come to a sad close. Julia goes back to her family, and Michael is left only with memories to torment him. Grief-stricken, he leaves the Maggoire Quartet. He is partly consoled when he learns that the old, invaluable Italian violin, lent to him by Mrs. Formby, his benefactor, has finally been gifted to him in her will.

The title is taken from a sermon by John Donne, where he is describing life after death. In heaven there will be "no sun, nor darkness nor dazzling, but one equal light, no noise nor silence, but one equal music." Regarding the epigraph, John Carey says, "But an epigraph might have been taken from another great English poet, Tennyson: "Deep as first love, and wild with all regret." Seth's story of love and loss can hold its own in the vicinity of that marvellous line."[12]

Thematically, these novels are no less authentic than the bhasa literature ('bhasa literature' is a cover term used by G.N. Devy and supported by Meenakshi Mukherjee for regional Indian literatures). One simply does not become less Indian if he/she writes in English. The themes employed by Vikram Seth bear Indian sensibility in the changing times and are authentic in tone and temperament. These novels clearly show the notion of 'hybridity' so assiduously built by the postcolonial critic Homi K. Bhabha. A discerning reader gets not only engrossed in the themes but participates in them with empathy. Therein lies the strength of Vikram Seth as Indian English writer.

NOTES

1. John Hollander, *The New Republic 1955* (2 April, 1896), p. 32.
2. X.J. Kennedy, *Los Angeles Times Book Review*, 6 April 1986.
3. Magonie Perloff, "Homeward Ho! Silicon Valley Pushkin," *American Poetry Review* (Nov.-Dec, 1986), pp. 137-46.
4. Vikram Seth, *The Golden Gate* (Delhi: Oxford University Press, 1992), p. 6.

5. Santosh Gupta, "The Golden Gate: The First Indian Novel in Verse," *The New Indian Novel in English*, ed. Viney Kirpal (New Delhi: Allied, 1990), p. 98.
6. Vikram Seth, *A Suitable Boy* (Delhi: Viking, 1993).
7. Rita Joshi, "The Novel of Our Times," *The Hindustan Times*, 27 Feb. 1993, p. 14.
8. Richard Woodward, "What Does *The New York Times* Think of Vikram Seth," *Parade* (September 1993), pp. 24-27.
9. Anita Desai, "Sitting Pretty," *New York Review of Books*, 41:10 (27 May, 1993), p. 23.
10. Vikram Seth, *An Equal Music* (Delhi: Penguin India, 1999).
11. John Carey, "Vikram Seth's music for the mind," *The Sunday Times*, April 2, 1999.
12. Ibid.